SADDLEWORTH
BUILDINGS

To Kit.

SADDLEWORTH BUILDINGS

A Guide to the Vernacular Architecture of the Parish of Saddleworth in the Pennines

W. JOHN SMITH, M.A., F.S.A.

SADDLEWORTH HISTORICAL SOCIETY
in Association with
The Saddleworth Festival of The Arts
1987

Published by Saddleworth Historical Society
in association with Saddleworth Festival of The Arts, 1987.

ISBN 0 904982 06 8

Printed by The Commercial Centre Ltd.
Hollinwood, Oldham.

Contents

Foreword

We are constantly reminded that the world is getting smaller as satellites beam images from one part of the globe to another almost instantaneously and as jet-powered planes make Dallas and Delhi seem as close as Dorchester and Dunfermline. Yet, paradoxically, there is a greater and greater interest in local studies as the familiar sights and sounds of once stable communities give us points of reference which we strive to maintain within the global uniformity. This is especially true of vernacular architecture, the dialect of buildings, and makes the appearance of this volume so timely.

The large parish of Saddleworth is a classic site for local study: accessible to visitors but not on a well-worn tourist route, changing economically and socially but at a gradual rather than a revolutionary pace, forming part of the current architectural scene but retaining a big proportion of the buildings which were erected during a period of economic flourish and architectural confidence. The signs of the local building history are there for all of us to see once our eyes are properly directed. There is no-one better qualified to remove the scales of architectural confusion from our eyes than Mr W. John Smith. Over years, almost decades, he has been carrying out research, carefully and deliberately, into the vernacular architecture of Saddleworth Parish. He has brought to this local study his wide knowledge of architecture in general and of the north-western quarter of England in particular. Over the years he has been sharing his discoveries with the people of Saddleworth through lectures and extra-mural courses. Now the time has come for him to draw together his investigations and publish his conclusions in this welcome volume.

We now have a reliable guide to the vernacular architecture of this Pennine parish. The residents will have a guide to their explorations of their neighbourhood. Those restoring old buildings will have a guide to the traditional solutions to problems which still remain with us. The visitors will have a guide to the tremendous architectural resources of Saddleworth so that their visits will be as rewarding as they should be frequent. I heartily recommend this volume as a worth-while introduction to an important subject by an author whose authority spills gently from his pen.

R. W. BRUNSKILL
School of Architecture
University of Manchester

April, 1987.

Preface

The purpose of the guide is to follow the development of building traditions in Saddleworth from the late sixteenth century to the early nineteenth century, relating building changes to the needs and aspirations of the inhabitants, and external cultural and economic influences.

A selection of buildings has been used to trace this development, but no attempt has been made to include a mention of every building built in Saddleworth before the mid-nineteenth century. This would have defeated the principal object of the present work which is given in its secondary title. But the information and views contained herein will make it possible to evaluate and appreciate a Saddleworth building and give guidance to further investigation of the architectural heritage of Saddleworth.

In view of the above, argument and discussion have been kept to the minimum, there is little in the way of quantitive analysis and at the moment of writing no systematic study has been made of the surviving wills and inventories relating to the Parish. This will be done and with the continued support and co-operation of Saddleworthians past, present and future will enable me to produce a definitive study of the vernacular architecture of Saddleworth.

No apology is offered for the plans and elevations of the buildings being given a scale in imperial units; they were built to these measurements. With a number of plans where there is a progression of building additions and alterations the first build is indicated by a bold line and the succeeding phases of building by progressively lighter lines.

Acknowledgements

I am grateful to Julian Hunt, Michael Buckley and the late Bernard Barnes for information which has had to be condensed out of necessity, and to Alan Petford for posing the right questions from time to time.

Julian Hunt and Alan Petford also worked hard to prepare the material for publication; their tact and gentle persuasive measures are here acknowledged with gratitude.

To the contributors to the *Saddleworth Historical Society Bulletin* I also owe a debt and I hope that this acknowledgement will be received by each one in the spirit that is intended.

I have been very fortunate in gaining the confidence of many owners of Saddleworth buildings which has enabled me to spend some time in their homes measuring up, and many have remained good friends. My thanks to you all, even if your particular house has not featured in this Guide, the experience helped me to come to some sound conclusion. I can recommend the tea and cakes and sometimes other refreshments offered and gratefully accepted on these occasions, and I hope this will continue for me in the future!

My thanks to the Librarian, Chetham's Library, Manchester for permission to reproduce the George Shaw drawings, to Peter Fox for the photograph of Shaw Hall, and to the Local Studies Centre, Oldham, for the print of the interior of Deanhead, c.1910.

The classes I have organised and run for the Extra-Mural Department of Manchester University have enabled me to learn more about Saddleworth than could be obtained from books. I am particularly pleased to acknowledge the help and advice over many years from Don Pemberton, mason, who has attended nearly every course.

To the late Harold and Nellie Ashton I am for ever indebted for their kind friendship and for introducing me to Saddleworth nearly thirty years ago.

And finally to my wife, Kit, for her supportive interest over many years of what began as a leisurely persuit.

Chapter 1.   The Setting

It is written in Greek on a boulder at Dovestones:

"Behold the Works of God." [1]

Saddleworth is a parish contained within the watershed of the upper River Tame and its tributaries the Diggle, Hull, Chew and Brun Brooks, and their dependencies. The southern boundary follows the county boundary.

The whole forms part of the Mid-Pennines lying to the west of the principal watershed. Politically it has long been part of Yorkshire being within the Honour of Wakefield, conversely it was once part of the vast parish of Whalley in Lancashire and later the parish of Rochdale. But geographically and geologically it belongs to both.

The area lies within a belt of millstone grit, a carboniferous sandstone laid down 400 million years ago. The landscape presents smoothly swelling slopes with ling-carpeted moors often capped by 'edges' and gashed by deep, steep groughs cutting through the peat to the bedrock beneath. The edges declare the rock beneath the pastures and open moor, millstone grit, a tough, coarse grained rock composed of broken down igneous rocks and quartz deposited as sand hundreds of millions of years ago, cemented under pressure with carbonate of silica, iron oxide and other agencies.[2] The rock is deeply fissured by joints and is prone to fracturing and weathering along the horizontal bedding planes, which has made it a convenient source for building materials.

On exposure to the effects of time and the weather the gritstone breaks down to produce a sandy soil which is acidic and of poor fertility. Valuable minerals and humus are washed down through the quartz grains that remain, so pasture is poor unless helped by the use of lime or marling. But the sandy soil and the underlying rock structure do provide good drainage off the moors and a good supply of soft water in the valleys.[3]

The millstone grits comprise sandstones alternating with soft shales and mudstone. In Saddleworth, as with the greater part of the adjoining moorlands to the north, west and south, it is the Kinder Scout Grits that lie beneath the open moors often breaking out to create the distinctive edges such as the awe-inspiring craggs at Dovestones. This Kinder Scout Grit rests on the Yoredale Rocks which consist of alternating layers of shales and sandstones, the former beds of shale being represented by the 'benches' or platforms along the valley sides. Some of these benches are very narrow, being merely a few yards wide while others extend up to half a mile from the gritstone scarp to the edge of the platform, as at Running Hill.

Because of the intervening bands of shales between beds of gritstone, spring lines appear along the valley sides and were no doubt instrumental in deciding the pattern of settlement from the thirteenth century.

The platforms are covered with glacial boulder clay with deposits of alluvium along the valleys. In some areas east of the Tame valley the boulder clay has been deposited in thicknesses of up to fifty feet. This clay contains pebbles, boulders and fragments of sandstones and grits which are of local derivation but must have been transported some distance from their source by glacial action.

In contrast the upland areas and moors, which are mainly in the east, are covered with a thick layer of peat on top of the grits. The beds of peat are furrowed with meandering groughs cut through the peat by water as it drains away down the cloughs to the brooks and ultimately to the river.

The thick soft spongy peat has preserved the remoteness of these barren moors which serve as poor sheep grazing and have in recent years also become the realm of the fell walker. A traveller writing in the *Bristol Journal* in 1766 described the area as,

". . . exceedingly populous though a barren and mountainous spot."[4]

whilst the Commercial Directory in 1817 wrote the parish down as being a,

". . . wild and bleak region."[5]

Cherryclough

Castleshaw Moor

Crompton Moor

Denshaw

Standedge

Delph
Slack

Higher Slack

Castleshaw

Bleak Hey
Nook

Oakdene
Deanhead

New
Tame

Marled
Earth

St. Thomas'

Grains Bar

Edge Hill

Higher Barn

Grange

Hull Brook

Harrop Green

Linfitts

River Tame

Dale

Digglee

Diggle Brook

Beswicks

Delph
Knott Hill

New Delph

Gatehead

Woolroad

Running Hill

Dobcross

Holy Trinity

St. Chads

Saddleworth
Fold

Old Parsonage

Uppermill

Higher
Cross

Saddleworth
Moor

Shaws

Knowl

Rye Top

Stonebreaks

Grasscroft

Grotton Hall

Shaw Hall

Tunstead

Boarshurst

Springhead Grotton

Lydgate

Hollins

St. Anne's

Thornlee

Windy Nook

Greenfield

Chew Brook

Woolleys

Hey Top

Quick Edge

Wellihole

0   ½   1 mile

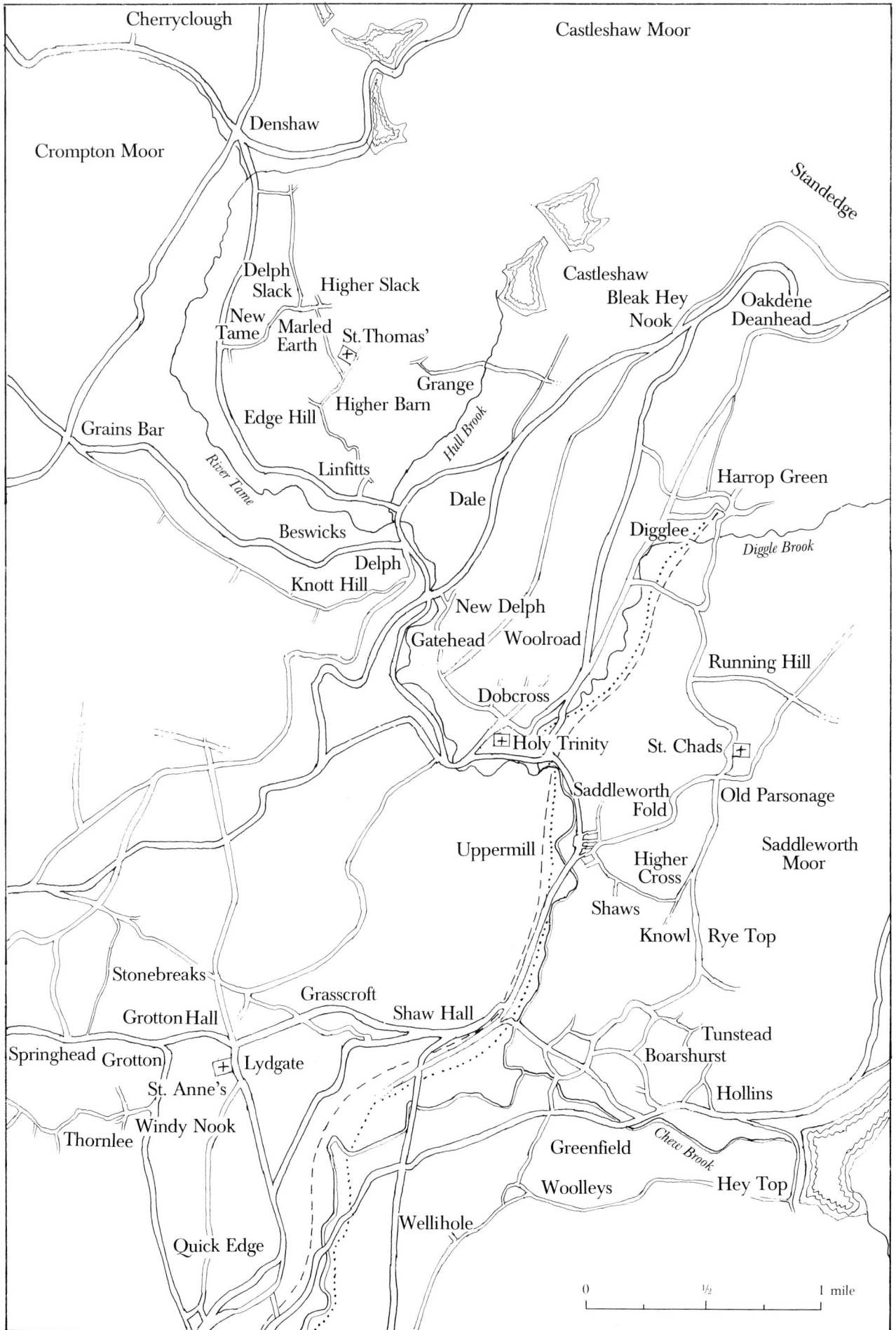

Map showing locations of places mentioned in the text.

Remote though the area appears to have been, settlement was established quite early mainly on the more gentle slopes on the eastern sides of the Upper Tame Valley which could also be easily cleared of forest. The population was large enough at the opening of the thirteenth century to need a chapel of ease to St. Chads at Rochdale, and this was provided by William Stapleton the Lord of the Manor circa 1215, who would no doubt also see the founding of a chapel as a mark of prestige.

Sixty years later a descendant, Robert Stapleton, provided land as an endowment for the chapel and this land included a 'toft to provide a competent manse in this place'. This land now forms the glebeland centred on Gellfield Lane and where the seventeenth century former vicarage now stands, presumably on 'the toft'. In 1292 the same Robert granted to the Abbey of Roche near Rotherham in Yorkshire, the whole of Friarmere.[6] This was then either farmed for the Abbey and a grange established on their estate, or more likely, the land was leased to local farmers. This association is remembered by the place-name of Grange, a small hamlet of late seventeenth and early eighteenth century houses and barns.

Both these sites, the Church and Grange, are between seven and eight hundred feet above sea level and other long established settlement sites are at a similar altitude, such as Saddleworth Fold and Hollingreave. Here the ground was dry, sheltered and had a good supply of water from springs and was well above the wooded and marshy valley bottom.

Following the Conquest, the Manor of Quick – the early name for the area now known as Saddleworth – was owned by Roger de Poictou and descended to the Stapletons around 1150. However no manorial lord ever established a manor house in Saddleworth and throughout the succession of the manor this situation did not change. The manor passed to the Ramsdens of Longley near Huddersfield, who sold it in 1654 to William Farrer of Ewood near Mytholmroyd, for £2,950.[7] The Farrers held it until 1791 when the majority of the tenants purchased their freeholds at a five day auction. What was left, including the manorial rights, was purchased by a group of local businessmen who thus became the '31 lords of the Manor'.

Apart from the Chapel, place names and the line of the old roads through Saddleworth,[8] there is very little to show the quality of life on the shelves between the bleak moors and marshy valley bottoms before the early seventeenth century.

Ridge piece — Collar

Purlin —

Wall plate —

Cruck blade —

Rearing hole —

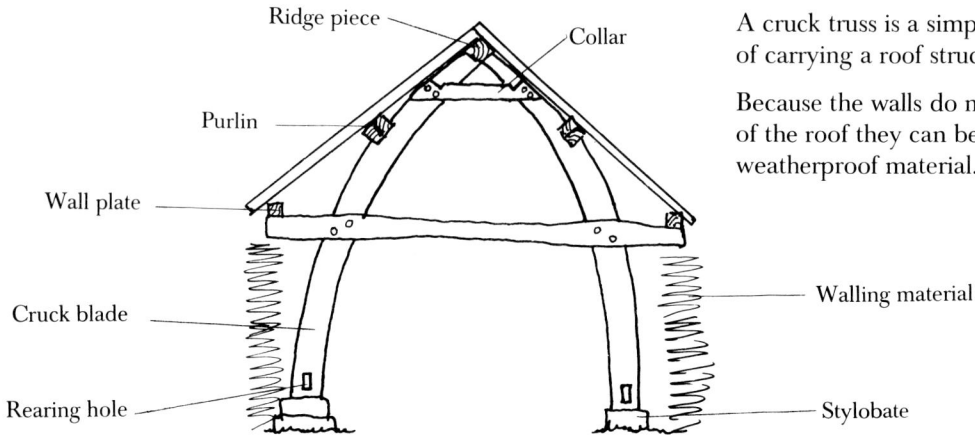

A cruck truss is a simple but strong way of carrying a roof structure.

Because the walls do not carry the weight of the roof they can be made of any weatherproof material.

— Walling material

— Stylobate

Half-lap joint securing the tie-beam to the blade.

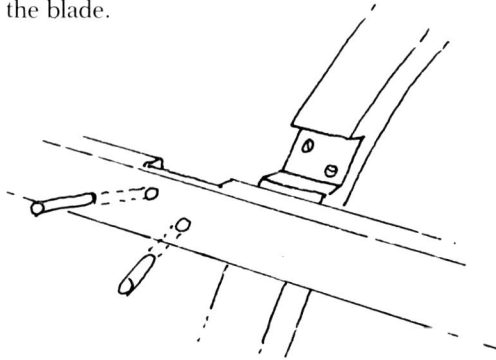

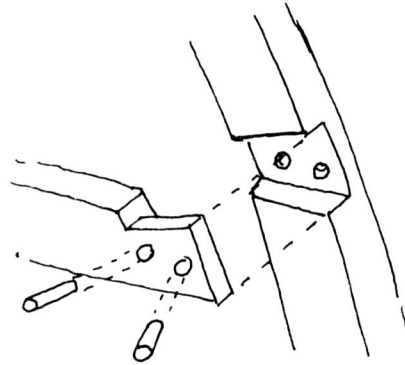

Half-lap dovetail to secure the collar to the upper part of the cruck blades.

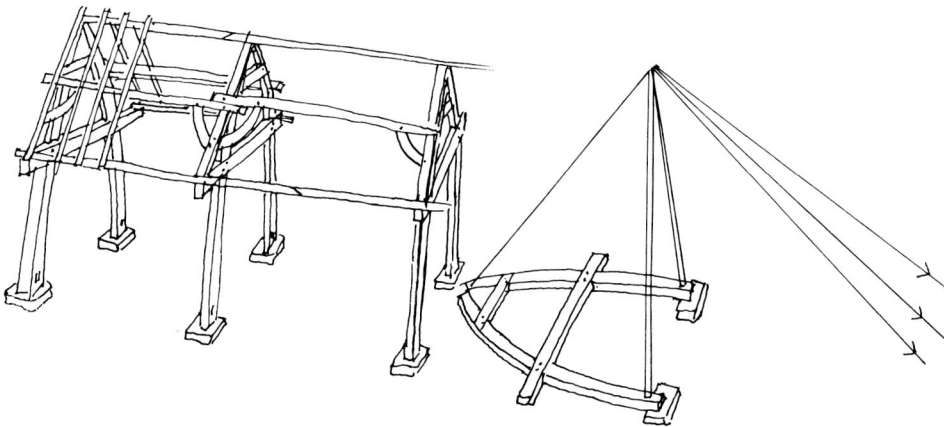

Raising a cruck-framed building. When each truss is raised it is held upright by poles until the purlins and wallplates can be assembled and braced to the truss. Note how the purlins overlap at each inner truss.

Features of a cruck truss.

14

Chapter 2.   Buildings Before The 17th Century

An engraving published in 1816 shows the old St. Chads church in Saddleworth which had by then been repaired, added to and partially rebuilt.[9] The tower was certainly rebuilt in 1746. Not surprisingly the church was built in stone and there is a quaint legend relating to the first building. This tells of elves or fairies removing stones from the original intended location at Brownhill, and taking them to their present site.[10] In this legend is the story of settlement, how upon experience the best site was found for a very important building to become the focus of a scattered community. Here the ground was dry, sheltered, with a good supply of water (there are copius wells in Church Bank Clough still), clear of the unsuitable lower lying lands and on one of the important ancient routes through Saddleworth. A better site could not be found.

But how were the people of the parish housed in the Middle Ages? There was no resident Lord of the Manor or his agent, so in their absence the incumbent of St. Chads would have been looked upon as the figurehead of the community and no doubt lived in a superior type of dwelling. Even if he was not fully resident in practice a suitable home would be provided for him, but nothing remains of his house, the manse on the toft. The houses and outhouses built by the community did not make use of durable materials like the church, and no doubt followed the practice common to many areas in the north and especially the upland areas — the tradition of cruck construction using the native oak.

While no complete cruck-frame building survives, two trusses have lately been discovered in the walls of later stone buildings. Cruck blades were often re-used as rafters from the mid-seventeenth century and short lengths of blades used as inner lintels of windows and doors.

A drawing made in the 1830's by George Shaw of Uppermill, shows a building in Boarshurst with two cruck trusses presumably still standing then,[11] but before comment is made on this drawing the background to cruck building needs to be given.

The tradition of cruck building is old and complex and its origins are obscure, both in date and location.[12] What is clear is that there is evidence enough to point to the cruck tradition of building being firmly established before the seventeenth century in Saddleworth.

This technique of building would be most suitable in Saddleworth which was rich in natural building materials — timber and stone. But it has also to be realised that social status played its part in the use of materials, especially from the late medieval times. Permanence of tenure was a rare thing, leases and grants of land were made but with limitations on the length of time and with obligations to certain dues and actions expected of the lessee. The cruck building provided a good shelter that could easily be constructed, and dismantled, and made a good economic use of the building materials available.

The general principle of cruck-framed building is to support a strong roof covering by cruck trusses spaced at intervals, the trusses extending down to the ground and so supporting the roof independent of any wall. The walls could then be built from any weather resistant material ranging from clay, timber frame to stone, depending on what was easily available locally, leaving openings for doorways and windows. The size of cruck trusses obviously vary, but the general dimensions were eighteen feet wide at the base, a similar height and with wall plates six to seven feet above ground level.

The cruck truss employed the use of the strongest and most stable structural form, the triangle. Place an equilateral triangular structure on its base, extend the two sloping sides from the base to the ground and you have a cruck truss. The sides can be straight, curved or wavy; can be matched pairs or dissimilar, but the resulting structure will always be strong. The apex of the truss is held by a yoke, or collar,[13] which can also help in giving support to the ridge piece. The tiebeam — the lower part of the triangle, spaces the cruck blades

Drawing by George Shaw of a cruck-framed building in Boarshurst.

and then is extended beyond the blades to a point above the feet of the blades to form the seating for the wallplates. These support the lower ends of the rafters and provide some stability for the upper part of the walling.

Jointing of the sections of the cruck truss is also basic and strong. The 'half-lap' and 'half-lap dovetail' joints are used exclusively. These joints require the use of simple tools, a saw, chisel and auger, and of course craftsmanship. The halved joints are held together by wooden pegs, or trennails, but first the joints are assembled on the ground then the peg holes are drilled with an auger, usually three per joint. These holes are rarely drilled to a parallel axis and if they are it is a sign of deteriorating standards of building. If the pegs are parallel then the joint can be easily opened but if the holes are drilled at angles varying to one another, with the joints in position and the pegs driven home, the resulting joints are tight and fast and will remain so for centuries unless or until the building is to be taken down, and then one has only to withdraw the pegs.

The practice of dismantling cruck trusses for rebuilding elsewhere or storage was an accepted practice nationally and the following extract from the Will of Arthur Schofield may refer to this practice. In 1557, Arthur Schofield of Schofield near Hollingworth in the parish of Rochdale, left to his son Christopher,

". . . vjs lodes of timber in Quyche and on paire of crockes lyeing in the maister lawe . . ." [14]

At this date the Schofields did not own land in Saddleworth so the probability is that Arthur Schofield had purchased timber in Saddleworth shortly before his death. What is clear from this gift is that timber – and crucks – were considered as valued properties for passing on to kinsfolk in the sixteenth century. [15]

Cruck trusses were simple to raise. First they were assembled on the ground and their feet placed on stone plinths which helped to preserve the timber from the wet and dampness in the ground. Using a simple lever principle of a long pole secured in a socket cut in the foot of each blade and then joined at their apex with ropes leading to the apex of the truss lying on the ground, the truss could then be pulled upright onto the stylobates and stabilised by props while the companion truss was raised in the same way, usually at a distance of eighteen to twenty feet between each truss.

Ridge piece, purlins and wall plates would then be laid across the bay now formed and secured to each truss. Braces from the purlins to the trusses would ensure lateral stability and this having been done the next truss or trusses could be reared and assembled in the same way. When all the trusses had been assembled and reared the walls could then be built and the roof covered with thatch or stone slates. Both materials were in use in Saddleworth in the later seventeenth century.

In the Raines manuscripts is a drawing by George Shaw of Uppermill referred to previously, showing the hall of a house once at Boarshurst in Saddleworth. It has long since gone and the site is no longer known with any certainty. The note to the drawing goes on to say

". . . the room, which was probably the hall, stands upon crooks, open to the roof, which are doubtless the remains of an original house, built at an early period of wood and plaster".

This drawing needs to be used with caution. Shaw often embellished his drawings for his friend F. R. Raines, then incumbent of Milnrow, adding to remains or decorating the structure according to his imagination as in the case of Shaw Hall. The drawing shows two cruck trusses, the nearer having both a yoke and collar but no tie-beam and the walling of the building appears to be largely independent of the trusses, only making use of the ridge. The other truss shows only the blades. The fireplace shown in the far gable end is a typical Saddleworth example of circa 1740, [16] while the spice cupboard to its left suggests a former inglenook at that end. The fireplace and spice cupboard are no doubt correct in appearance when the drawing was done, but the crucks may well have only partially remained, perhaps just discernable in partition walls of a later period, and Shaw reconstructed them to what he thought was their original appearance.

The value of the drawing is that it supports the idea that there was a cruck frame tradition in Saddleworth. These trusses must have been in a poor state which Shaw corrected in his limited way, hence the anomolies such as the lack of tiebeams, purlins and bracing.

In more recent times two cruck trusses have been discovered in Saddleworth and both are fairly complete. The best example is at Lane Farm, Grotton, discovered incorporated into a late eighteenth century brick partition wall. The other is in the dividing wall between two cottages at New Tame, where it is partially obscured by the stone wall surrounding it. Both sets of blades are wavy and both have a collar and yoke as well as a tiebeam.

Re-used portions of cruck blades are used in the roof truss at Windy Nook, Grotton (1648) and at Lower Cottage, Nicker Brow, Dobcross, built in 1742. The period of replacing cruck truss houses was very long. The Old Parsonage House on Gellfield Lane has two sections of cruck blades acting as inner lintels behind the large stone lintel over the entrance. Remains of cruck trusses are acting as rafters in an outshut at Lower Grange. A complete collar has been discovered at Marden House, Denshaw where it had been acting as an inner lintel for a window; as well as having dovetail half-lap tenons, the open peg holes clearly show the divergent angles they were drilled. Fur Lane Cottage, rebuilt in the late seventeenth century, has a floor joist which was originally a purlin in which are two half-lap seatings for small braces.

More examples of the remains of cruck building features may yet come to light reinforcing the knowledge that the basic medieval tradition of building in Saddleworth, in common with the whole of the north west, was that of the cruck truss.

The two complete cruck trusses mentioned above reveal from their size that the buildings associated with them were of one storey with perhaps a small loft at one end.

The other tradition of building in timber, the box-frame structure, is not represented in Saddleworth whereas examples are found outside the area. Near Oldham they were to be found in the Failsworth area and one still survives at Woodhouses. Stubley Old Hall near Littleborough, has a cruck frame south wing and a later box-frame hall and north wing, all now encased in stone. In Middleton there are the Boar's Head Inn built circa 1632, and Tonge Hall built circa 1590, and near to the M62 is Lower Whittle, a newly discovered early seventeenth century timber-framed house of box-frame construction.

In a spirit of loyalty to his native heath and having a rudimentary knowledge of the vernacular architecture outside Saddleworth, George Shaw drew a reconstruction of Shaw Hall for Raines in the 1830's, giving it a decorative timber façade at first floor level in the central wing. This drawing has long been believed to be an accurate view of the hall, but this has now to be regarded as very doubtful indeed.[17]

Shaw's drawing is of a house with two short cross wings at either end of the central hall wing, with a short two bay wing on the right. The hall is represented as extending the full height of the building which is shown as being largely built of stone rising from a plinth, with mullion windows and a stone slated roof. Entrance is by a stone castellated porch with gargoyles at the corners. Running over the porch and over the two tall hall windows and along the full length of the hall, is the band of timber framing based on quatrefoil panels. Clearly this building was being made to appear venerable and socially high in status. But why? Perhaps in Shaw's mind he could still see the house being the one once in the possession of the Radcliffe family of Ordsall in Salford and continuing through minor branches of that family until about 1689 when it passed by marriage to the Whitehead family of Lydgate. A datestone on the barn to the south of Oldham Road, Grasscroft, is inscribed J^WA 1701. John Whitehead was the estate agent to the Farrers, Lords of the Manor since 1654, and so could be looked upon as amongst the leaders of Saddleworth society. By George Shaw's time, however, the group of buildings now known collectively as the Farrer's Arms had grown up at the junction of Oldham Road and Mossley Road and no

Roof truss in Lower Cottage, Nicker Brow, Dobcross. Note the curved rafters which were cruck blades. On the reverse side are half-lap joints, now empty, for the tie-beam.

Drawing by George Shaw of Shaw Hall, Grasscroft as he imagined it to have been.

doubt Shaw was of the opinion that these had replaced the old hall, a view repeated by Joseph Bradbury in 1871,[18] who also includes a copy of the Shaw drawing to which he gives the date of 1790 – which was the time when the new Oldham to Standedge Turnpike Road was being promoted.

Looking at the drawing three observations can be made. First, the style of fenestration, the gable kneelers, finials, small two-light gable windows, castellated porch and gargoyle water spouts, are all features found in the Rochdale, Littleborough area where Shaw made many drawings of buildings for Raines, notably one of the Holte, also shown with timber framing similar to that shown on Shaw Hall.[19] Secondly, the site of Shaw Hall lacks depth, the building platform is little more than thirty feet wide with a steep rise in the land behind and an equally steep fall in front of the hall. This was built up and broadened when the turnpike road was built. Yet the drawing shows four chimney stacks behind the hall wing which shows no upper floor, the suggestion then being that there was a substantial wing behind the hall which in retrospect seems unlikely in view of the restricted site. Thirdly, the timber framing. It can hardly be called 'framing' lacking as it does any vertical posts necessary to stabilise the structure. What we see is more akin to the mechanism of old-fashioned fire tongs. Clearly the building was a composite based on the infirm recollections of old Saddleworthians, or merely the grandiose allusions by Shaw to his possible ancestral home.

What may remain of Shaw Hall will be discussed later, but to summarise this section, little is known of remains of buildings in the period down to the end of the sixteenth century. That the cruck-frame tradition was widely used there is no doubt but the size of the houses or cottages, their planforms and outbuildings are not yet determined, neither documentary nor physical evidence being known. But judging from the way the Saddleworth house moved into its next phase, stone walls in association with cruck trusses must have become quite general by the sixteenth century. The steep pitch of the two surviving cruck trusses suggest a covering of thatch, perhaps of ling, and there are several references to ancient thatched buildings in the 1770 key to the map of Saddleworth.[20]

The social structure may not have been very wide, there was no resident family of manorial status and an agent acting for the Lords of the Manor appears at a later period. But a resident minister would no doubt have filled this gap, living on the glebe land with an income derived from tithes and rents, but in what kind of house?

Chapter 3.   Traditions established, 1600–1720

From a cruck-frame tradition Saddleworth moved into the total use of stone for building, dispensing with the cruck truss from the early seventeenth century. The quality of workmanship in these early seventeenth century buildings shows fully developed skills in using stone for building, presumably from the experience of using it to clad the cruck-frame buildings towards the end of the previous period.

The changes may well have been prompted by a desire to increase the accommodation and add to the comforts of the house by including an upper floor, a feature restricted by the cruck truss. It is tempting to credit this change to the Old Parsonage House on Gellfield Lane, built in the early seventeenth century, which from its social status as the home of the minister could have well been superior to others in the parish – for a time. But before describing this and some other early stone buildings in Saddleworth it is necessary to understand and appreciate the qualities of the local stone and the techniques involved in its use for building.

Depending on the situation of the building to the nearest natural resource, the basic material for the walls was flagstones or gritstones. But for the 'dressings', that is the corner stones (quoins), windows and doorways, the hard and intractable grit stone was invariably used until the later eighteenth century. Saddleworth was well endowed with both types of stone.

The stone would be quarried from the bedrock, laboriously cut from the grit stone or split in the case of flagstone. The stone would then be roughly dressed at the quarry, trimmed to a uniform depth with a face and upper bed chiselled to a flat plane ready for the mason and wallers.

Whatever the type of stone used to build the walls the construction was always the same, an inner and outer leaf or skin with a solid core. There was no open cavity. The stones for both inner and outer skins were cut, dressed and laid so that an unbroken vertical plane was achieved while the inner face of each skin would have the untrimmed end running back in varying lengths into the core. A lime and sand mortar was used to bed each course of stone and the joints between each stone and each course were made as fine as possible to limit water penetration.

The purpose of the core was two-fold, first to firmly anchor the inner ends of each walling stone so that it would not work loose, and secondly to provide a form of insulation for the occupants from the seasonal weather conditions. The core was a mixture of clay, daub and small stone chippings with bent (a tough moorland grass) or animal hair mixed in with it; this helped the mixture to hold together and not crumble and fall away. This technique can easily be seen in the wall sections of many Saddleworth buildings lying in ruins and built before the 1760's. If these have been open to the weather for long it can be seen that the core will have washed away so making a further section of wall unsafe.

At intervals walling stones were taken through the full width of the wall to act as bond stones helping to tie together the two skins and prevent the walls from bulging. From the outside it is not clear which stones in the wall are acting in this way, but looking at a section of broken walling they are unmistakeable.

The walls rise from a foundation of large flat-topped stones laid into the ground with their top surfaces at ground level. These foundations are not deep but are wider than the wall above.[21] Often a plinth from nine to fourteen inches high and two to four inches wider than the wall above, is first laid in order that a perfectly horizontal base can be made for the main wall. The wall is then laid in courses the depth of each course depending on the type of walling stone being used. Saddleworth is particularly fortunate in having stone that could be quarried or cut to regular dimensions. There are examples of various types of coursing found in Saddleworth, diminishing coursing at Windy Nook, irregular coursing

A typical Saddleworth window during the period 1630 to 1760. This example is at Woolleys, Greenfield.

Drawing by George Shaw of the Old Parsonage House, on Gellfield Lane. The porch has long since gone and a door is now in the gable end to the right of the chimney buttress. Note that Shaw has given the wrong number of windows to the parlour and chamber above.

at Bank Top and the Old Parsonage and regular coursing at the extension to Pinfold circa 1800.

At the corners of each section of wall are quoins or corner stones. These are carefully cut from gritstone and serve to give strength to the corners vulnerable to the weather and the clumsy passage of carts or sleds.

In common with other areas with stone building traditions the joints between the courses and each stone in the course are kept as fine as possible and in order to achieve this the top bed of each stone is worked to a flat bed while the under face could be left rough. The fine joints had to be on the face in order to restrict the amount of rain penetration into the wall through the joints. The mortar used to bed each stone was lime based and absorbed water during wet weather, which would later evaporate with the help of breezes and so cut down the risk of damp penetrating through the walls. Where this happens today it is caused by the wrong mix in repointing.

Walls were built to a width of eighteen to twenty-four inches, the earlier buildings having the wider measurement, and a two-storeyed building would rise fifteen feet to the eaves. The top surface of the walls was protected by the roofing material or, if this did not cover the top of the gable walls, by coping stones. This protection was vital for rainwater must be kept out of the core of the walls for obvious reasons.

Like quoins, the windows and doorways called for careful and precise masoncraft. The window opening was framed by a lintel supported at the sides by jambs which in turn stood on a sill. If the window was more than one foot three inches wide the opening would be divided into lights by mullions which had to be sturdy enough to carry the weight of the wall mass above them. So the use here of the tough, coarse gritstone not subject to the risk of splitting along bedding lines, can be appreciated. In order not to inhibit light passing through the window the jambs, mullions and lintels were splayed outwards. The sill was also splayed, but more to encourage the rain water to run off it.

In Saddleworth the section of this splay was 'cavetto', or a hollow chamfer. This is a little more sophisticated than plain chamfer and gives the mullions a less massive appearance. An interesting comment on the local culture. Only rarely are other mullion sections used before the 1790's.

> "The mullioned windows, splayed and deep,
> Attest the craftsman's skill," [22]

Sill, jambs and lintels were cut from stone which reached back often to the full depth of the wall, but the mullions only average nine inches in depth or less than half the width of the wall and they are not placed directly in the central axis of the wall but nearer the outer face of the wall. This makes possible a continuous sill on the inside of the window while outside the face of the mullions are set three to four inches back from the vertical plane of the outer wall. This 'set back' is echoed in both jambs and in the lintel by an inner, or lower, lintel immediately over the mullions. This feature continues in Saddleworth right through the whole period of this study.

The doorways have built-up jambs, keyed into the wall like quoins. They are usually two feet ten inches wide on the outside opening, then there is a rebate for the door – this acts as a weather seal, and the opening then splays out to give a width of up to three feet six inches. The jambs carry a lintel which is a monolith and on this the date and initials of a proud owner or builder are often cut.

> "Its rude doorhead is graven with
> A bygone yeoman's name;" [23]

Unlike the windows, door lintels are not always the full depth of the wall, occasionally there are two or three lintels behind each other to the full depth of the wall, often these inner lintels are a massive piece of oak. In the Old Parsonage House this inner lintel is made from two sections of former cruck blades, recognisable by their dimensions and curvature.

Timber was mainly used for the floor joists and roof trusses and it was the heart of the oak that was used. The floor joists were built in as the walls rose, spanning each room from gable to gable via an internal wall which was either of timber or stone. These joists averaged nine inches wide and twelve inches deep, the lower edges were chamfered, a simple decorative feature which had its origins in the way the sapwood, prone to decay, was cut away from the more resilient heartwood. The chamfers have a simple splay and have shoulder stops just before the joist enters the wall. Secondary joists are housed along the upper edge of the main joists and fit into prepared sockets in the wall, any space being filled up with stone flakes and plaster. Floorboards were wide, up to fifteen inches, and were pegged to the joists beneath fitting edge to edge. As they were made from the oak sapwood most such floorboards have long since decayed and have been replaced.

Staircases were simple, in common with other adjacent regions, the ladder stair was no doubt used or a plank ladder in the smallest cottages.

Until the late eighteenth century roof trusses were not common in Saddleworth. The cross walls, most of which are of stone, rise to the full height of the building and follow the form of the end gables. Purlins resting on these gable walls, usually two each side, carry the common rafters which are secured at their apex on to the ridge piece, also of oak. Many of these purlins are very roughly prepared, branches lopped off with slight attempt to square them off, and in some instances the bark is still surviving. Forked trees are not infrequently found with the junction of the fork being clearly visible as it goes into the wall.

Apart from the two cruck trusses already mentioned, the earliest known roof truss is at Windy Nook, built in 1648. This is a tie-beam rafter truss – a triangle of substantial timbers, once cruck blades, with the base – the tie-beam – extended into the side walls. At Lower Grange (1659) there is a collar tie-beam truss with side braces.

From the early seventeenth century the roof covering was of flagstone available from local quarries which exposed the Elland Flag series.[24] These stones can be split into narrow smooth flags of constant thickness. The sizes vary, with the larger flags being laid at the eaves to cover the full width of the wall and the courses gradually narrowing up to the ridge which is covered by a ridge piece cut from gritstone. This is an inverted 'V' in section and was kept deliberately heavy to avoid being disturbed by high winds and snow.

At the eaves the flags were laid double, the second course being laid to cover the joints of the first course. This was to give complete weather protection to the open top of the wall. The flags had holes bored through near the top edge and an oak dowel used to hang the flag on the laths spanning the rafters. Finally, the back of the flags on the completed roof were plastered to keep rain and snow from being blown under the flags and into the house. This plaster was mixed with hair to prevent it breaking up and falling away. An alternative was to use moss which was pushed under the lower edges of the flags from the outside. This had the advantage of not being disturbed and falling away with the slight movement of the flags in heavy winds. This practise continued in Saddleworth until 1823.[25]

Internally the walls, door jambs and lintels, window sills, jambs, lintels and mullions would have been plastered to give a smooth surface and then whitewashed. The lower coats of whitewash existing until recently at Lower Grange were white but later coats are of a light blue colour. This was a lime wash but with copper sulphate added as an insect deterrent. This was a widespread practice from the early eighteenth century until the early decades of the present century.

The front of the Old Parsonage House. To the right of the downpipe is the additional bay.

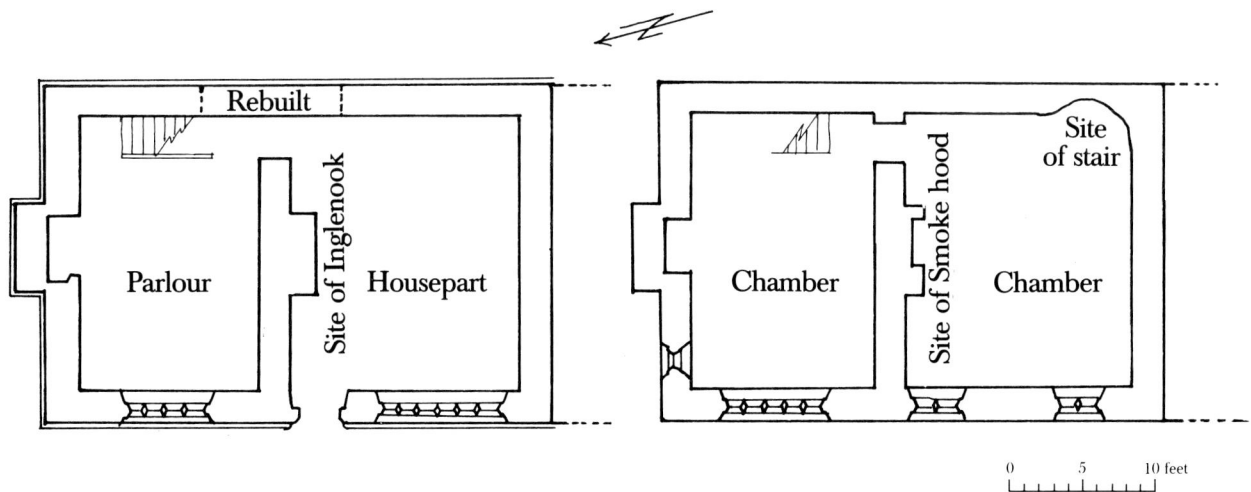

Plan of the Old Parsonage House.

Some Examples of Early Stone Buildings in Saddleworth

While there are several datestones before the 1640's recorded in Saddleworth, few of the buildings associated with them survive.[26] What is probably the earliest surviving stone building in Saddleworth is that long known as the Old Parsonage House on Gellfield Lane, one of the ancient routes through the district. It is described in the *Glebe Terrier* of 1701 as,

> "A House with three Bays; an old Barn of three Bays one Stable one Shipon, A New Barn of two Bays which our present Minister hath erected upon his own proper Costs . . ."[27]

It is a two-storey gritstone building measuring thirty-four feet by twenty-two embodying the vernacular traditions of the upland stone region of the Pennines in the early seventeenth century.

Apart from it being of two units, the plan form is not typical of Saddleworth in relation to other and later stone buildings in the area and may be seen as an 'immigrant' type from over the watershed to the east. The full understanding of this building is complicated by changes made over the centuries. In the early eighteenth century when John Heginbottom began his time as minister of St. Chads, the house was in a poor condition and had to be repaired before he could live there with his family. His successor some fifty years later kept a school there and this may have accounted for more changes. The rear of the building has many vertical breaks in the masonry, changes of coursing and blocked windows. A door has been made in the north gable within the last hundred years.[28] Internally very little has survived from the seventeenth century apart from the fireplace in the north gable and two features which help reconstruct the interior of the past.

In the chamber over the housepart is a mid-eighteenth century fireplace with a narrow overmantle, set against the dividing cross wall which is the same thickness as the outside walls and rises to the full height of the roof. At the apex of this chimney flue there are two corbels supporting the stone stack as it passes through the roof. From this evidence it is very likely that there was a smoke hood rising from an inglenook fireplace in the housepart. The present housepart fireplace is modern. Entry into the house would then have been via a baffle entrance with a spere sheltering the inglenook, and making a lobby, with a door to the right leading into the housepart and a door to the left leading into the parlour. This is now blocked and entry is now via a doorway at the far end of the cross wall. At this point in the rear wall there is a break in the masonry where a fireside window for the inglenook would have been. This fireside window is a feature common to many Pennine houses from about 1600 to the early eighteenth century.[29]

In the south east corner of the housepart the inner face of the wall curves as if there had been a spiral staircase there giving the access to the upper chambers. This view is supported by what can be seen of the floor structure in this corner.

Architecturally the most significant features are the windows on the west front. On the ground floor there are two, a six-light window to the housepart and a four-light window to the parlour. Both windows have hood moulds with decorative stops, the parlour hood mould having dropped ends while the housepart window hood mould terminates in a simple stylised floral design of the 1630's. The upper floor windows have no hood moulds. The mullions are all cavetto in section.

In this description the rooms have been given a specific identity. Just as today the terms 'hallway', 'passage', 'kitchen', 'dining-room', 'drawing-room', and 'lounge' identify specific functions for the rooms in a house so it was centuries ago. From a study of inventories, a document drawn up to establish probate of the estate of a testator, all possessions formerly belonging to him (or her) were recorded by appraisers who occasionally listed the rooms together with their contents. From this we find that the main room was referred to as the 'house', 'housepart', 'dwellinghouse' or 'firehouse' but rarely as the 'hall'. In this guide the term 'housepart' is used to avoid confusion. Next to it would be the 'parlour' and the

Rear view of the Old Parsonage House. The disturbed masonry under the two-light window shows the position of the former fireside window.

Door and six-light window to the housepart of the Old Parsonage House. Between the two upper windows can be seen the sill of a former three-light window.

The parlour window of the Old Parsonage House showing the hood mould. Note the plinth, and varied coursing of the wall.

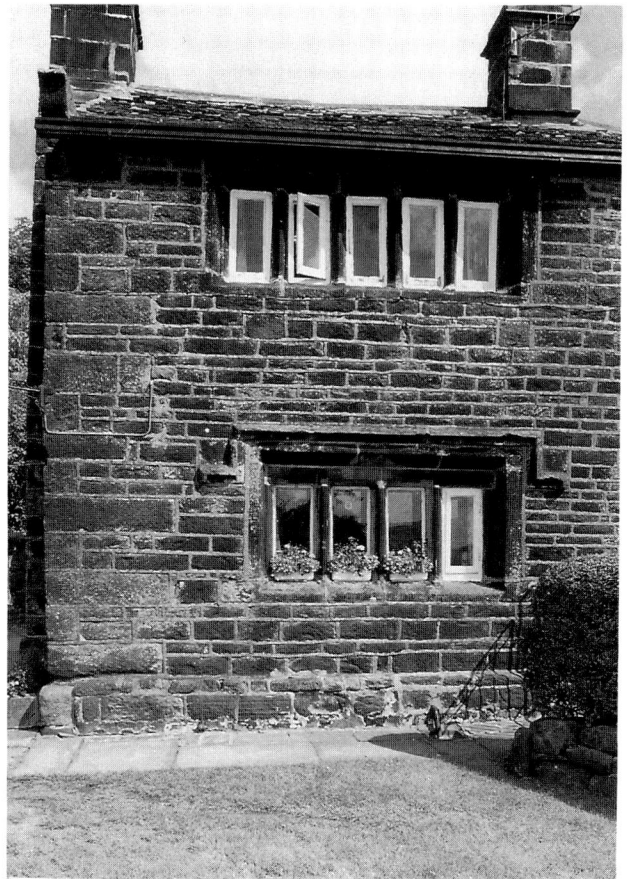

Decorative stop on the hood mould over the housepart window.

Windy Nook, Grotton. The south front. To the left of the quoin stones is the mid-eighteenth century kitchen and chamber.

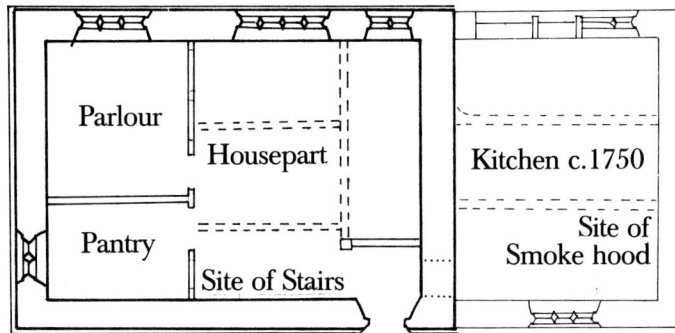

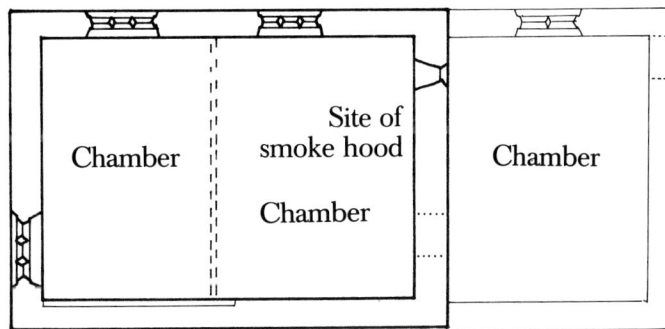

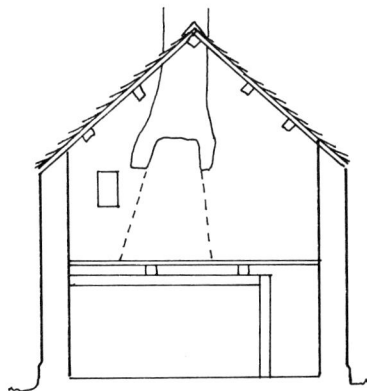

Plan and cross-section of Windy Nook.

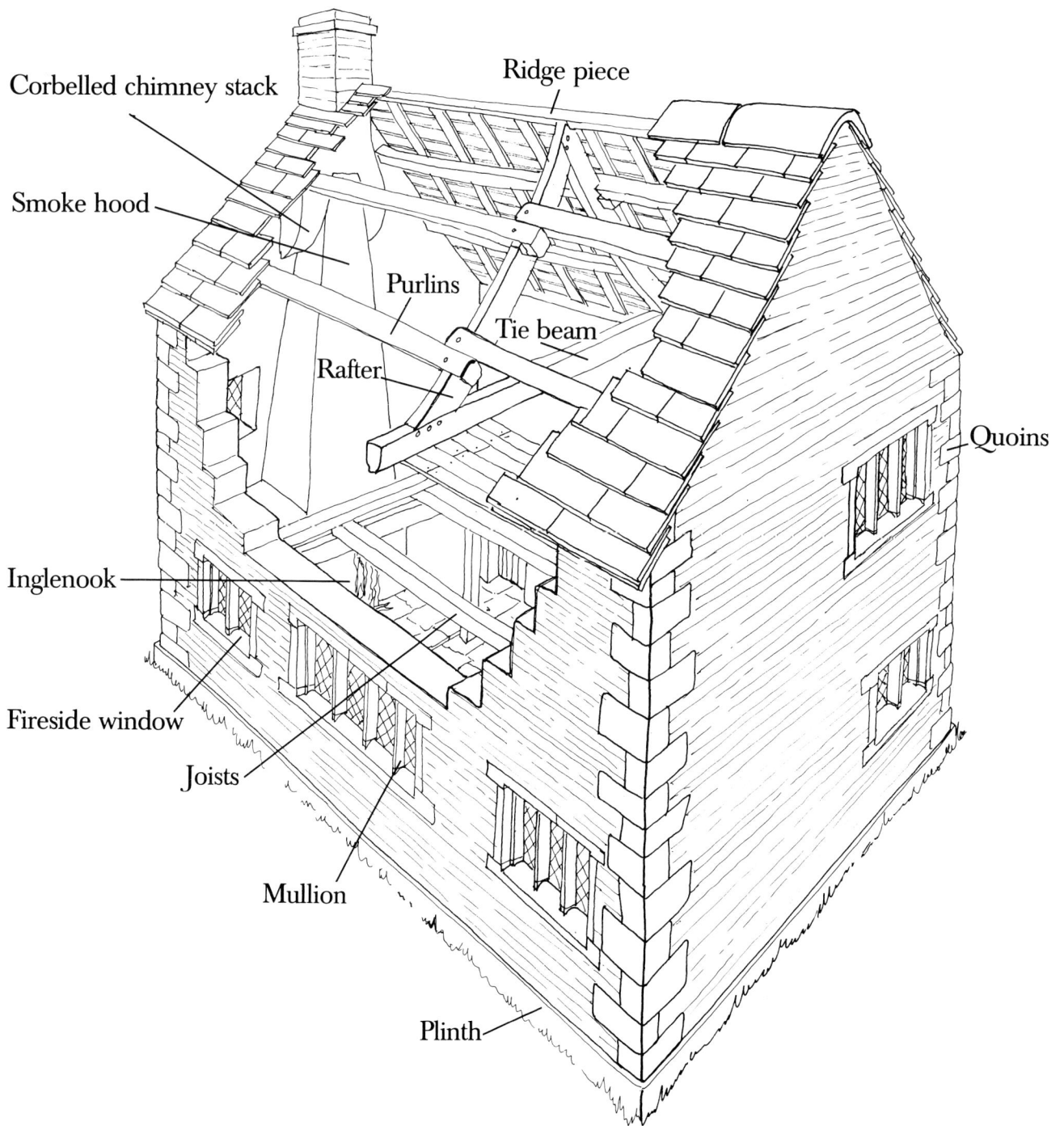

Corbelled chimney stack

Smoke hood

Ridge piece

Purlins

Tie beam

Rafter

Quoins

Inglenook

Fireside window

Joists

Mullion

Plinth

Cut-away diagram of Windy Nook showing the former inglenook and smoke hood.

Entrance with dated lintel on the north side of Windy Nook.

Windy Nook. Internal timber-framed partition wall during restoration. The wattle and daub infilling of the panels can be seen.

Windy Nook. Part of the corbelling supporting the chimney stack. The smoke-hood would have fitted between both corbels.

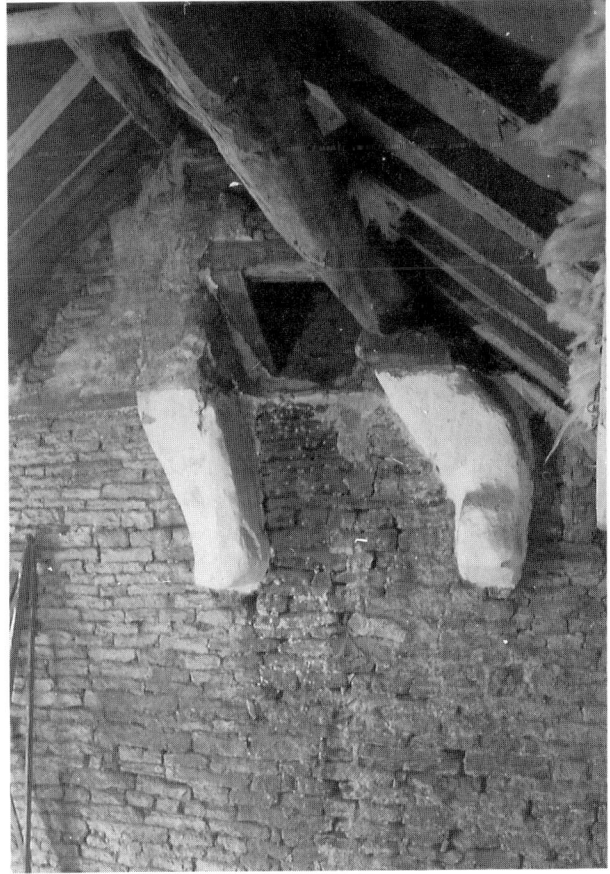
Windy Nook. Remains of smoke-hood and corbelling of chimney stack in the later kitchen.

'pantry'; occasionally the alternative term 'buttery' was used. 'Kitchens' are also mentioned. The upper rooms were usually distinguished by the name of 'chambers' or more specifically 'chamber over house', 'nearer chamber' or 'greater chamber'. There are occasional references to 'shop' which would have indicated a workplace.

The Old Parsonage has its share of problems of interpretation, but there are few with Windy Nook at Lane in Grotton and just within the Saddleworth boundary. The datestone on the deep lintel over the entrance proclaims that Henry Shaw built the house in 1648 and his successors continued to live there until late into the eighteenth century.

It is a small two bay house measuring twenty-nine feet by twenty-one, well built of the local flagstone with gritstone dressings. Internally the partition walls are of timber frame construction with wattle and daub panels plastered over, a common practice up to the early eighteenth century. The main front faces south but the entrance is on the north and was the only opening on that side.[30]

The plan form is very simple and was repeated in most houses built in Saddleworth for the next two hundred years. It is a two-bay plan with the housepart occupying one bay and the parlour plus pantry in the other smaller bay. The housepart is lit by a four-light mullion window plus a two-light window giving light to an inglenook. A three-light mullion window provides light to the parlour and two three-light windows give light to the two upper chambers. In the east gable were a two-light window to the pantry and in the floor above a three-light window, all with cavetto mullions. There are no hood moulds to any windows. In the west gable there was a single-light window at first floor level. Internally in this gable end is a feature similar to that found in the Old Parsonage, corbels for supporting a stone chimney stack above a wooden-framed smoke hood over the inglenook. Many Saddleworth houses built as late as the 1740's show signs of having had smoke hoods such as Oakdene Cottage at Deanhead, built circa 1742, and shortly before 1774 a smoke hood was part of a kitchen extension added to Windy Nook.[31] The inglenook has long since gone and the floor joists have been extended to reach the west gable.

The workmanship throughout is good, the building rising from a plinth and the walls built in gradually diminishing courses which show little sign of their age. The roof structure has already been mentioned.

The plan form is of the lobby entrance type which was no doubt determined by the position of the house to its site. To the south the ground falls away sharply down to a small brook. The platform on which the house stands extends north and along it runs an old trackway, so the natural approach to the house would be on that side. The house that Henry Shaw built at Windy Nook has survived remarkably unchanged and provides us with the best example of a yeoman's dwelling of this period in Saddleworth.

A similar house remains in part at Bank Top, just to the east of Gellfield Lane before it drops down to pass to the west of St. Chads Church. This is dated 1633 (or 1635, the last digit is very worn) on the deep lintel over the entrance. The similarity to Windy Nook extends to its dimensions, thirty by twenty feet, plan form, position of entrance and the two surviving windows. But over the years it has undergone many physical changes.

There was other building activity in Saddleworth at this period, in particular at Grotton Hall. Richard Buckley of Grotton in his Will dated 1633 had left the 'new land with edifices thereon' to his sons the eldest of whom received the family home. In 1635 this was described as a 'Capital Messuage at Grottonhead'. Little of this building survives. The Buckleys became a very wealthy and influential family in Saddleworth and not surprisingly improved their family home each generation – and this process has continued until the present – though the property left the Buckley family in 1912.[32] Grotton Hall represents the larger house in Saddleworth and may well have been the only one in this period.

Windy Nook and Bank Top are more representative of the better homes of

Drawing by George Shaw of Grotton Hall, circa 1830.

Saddleworthians – small, modest in design, stone built and showing an accomplished use of that material. In the absence of other examples built before the mid-seventeenth century, it must be assumed that the majority of the population were still living in the older buildings and would continue to do so until the later seventeenth century. However, datestone evidence points to some building activity among the wealthier yeomen in the mid-seventeenth century and one building survives largely intact at Lower Grange in the Castleshaw valley.

The hamlet of Grange has not been systematically surveyed or searched for remains of its monastic connection with Roche Abbey. It is very probable that the site of present day Grange has been settled since the thirteenth century with the settlers living in the basic house type previously described. To support this theory an outshut on the east side of Lower Grange has two rafters which have the distinctive curvature of cruck blades in addition to having vacant dovetail half-laps.

The earliest building is at the southern end of the row known as Lower Grange. On its south gable was once a datestone of 1659 recording the initials of John and Mary Scholefield who were married in 1658 at Ashton-under-Lyne. The house they built was modelled on recent precedents but was to differ in one significant feature – the position of the entrance. The general dimensions of the house have remained the same but earlier this century a new façade was given to the west front completely out of character with the rest. The south gable shows signs of changes too, but of an earlier period, and in this gable is the entrance into the house, surmounted by a triangular topped lintel, a type that was once fairly common in Saddleworth. This entrance would have led into the housepart alongside the spere of the inglenook, which has now gone, but its position can be gauged from where extensions were added to the joists in the late eighteenth century. The housepart was separated from the parlour and pantry by a timber-framed partition rising the full height to the tiebeam of the roof truss. This is a collar tiebeam truss with curved side braces. The partition is built of substantial posts and rails, the former are housed in prepared stone sockets in the floor with, between the posts, a low long stone grooved on its upper surface to house the stakes for the wattle and daub infil of the panels. A similar partition divided the parlour from the pantry but this division did not extend into the floor above. Of the two doorways in this dividing wall the one leading into the parlour still exists, and has a lintel with a decorative ogee scroll on the under surface. There was a similar example at Higher Barn Farm on Dark Lane, Delph, and two still survive at Rough Bank, Newhey, built in 1607.

In common with early Saddleworth two-unit plans, the parlour at Lower Grange was unheated. The present fireplace is an early nineteenth century addition. The pantry, roughly one-third the size of the parlour, was lit by two two-light mullion windows, without hood moulds but with cavetto section mullions. This pattern is also seen at Ralphs, Denshaw and at Shaw Fold, Stonebreaks, both buildings of the 1670's, and also at The Cottage, Running Hill, built in the early eighteenth century.

Lower Grange was innovative in another detail. On the inside of the east wall at ceiling height is a three inch ledge, the wall above being therefore that much narrower. This ledge would have made laying floor joists much easier within a stone shell and is evidence of an improving technique in building construction and maintenance. Other examples of this technique are to be found at Hollingworth Fold near Chorley, 1686 and at Old Bent House, Littleborough, built in 1692,[33] so perhaps for the first time Saddleworth may have been pioneering a new form of building construction.

On the east wall of the housepart end are two small single-light arched windows above each other. The lower one has some decorative carving on the lintel spandrels and some indecipherable lettering on an associated stone. The purpose of the two windows is not

Lower Grange. The west front was refaced between the Wars.

Lower Grange. The south gable showing the original entrance with its triangular lintel. The wall has been much disturbed.

Lower Grange. The original entrance.

Lower Grange. The scarf joint on one of the principle floor joists. These were extended when the inglenook bressumer beam was removed, c.1800.

Lower Grange. The collar tie-beam truss.

Lower Grange. Remains of timber-framed partition between the housepart and parlour. Note the ogee lintel to the doorway.

Lower Grange. The lower ends of the posts of the partition were supported by a low stone plinth, grooved to help hold the stakes for the wattle and daub infilling.

B

Site of Stair

Pantry

Site of Inglenook

Parlour

Housepart

Wall rebuilt

A

0   5   10 feet

Section A–B

0   5 feet

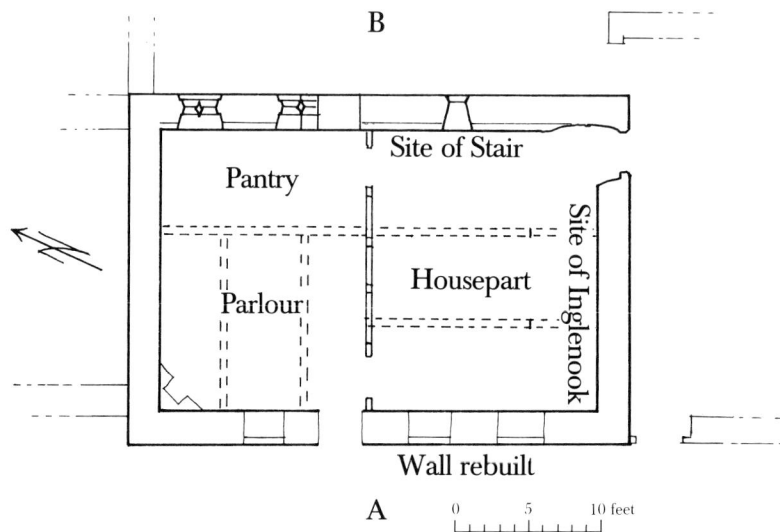

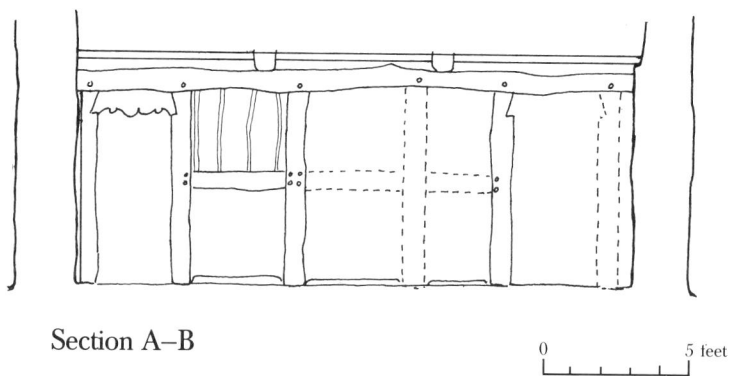

Plan of Lower Grange and elevation of internal partition.

Lower Grange. The east side showing the two single-light windows, one above the other, and the two three-light windows to the pantry beyond. A later doorway has cut through part of one window.

Lower Grange. The lower of the two single-light windows showing the very simple decorations.

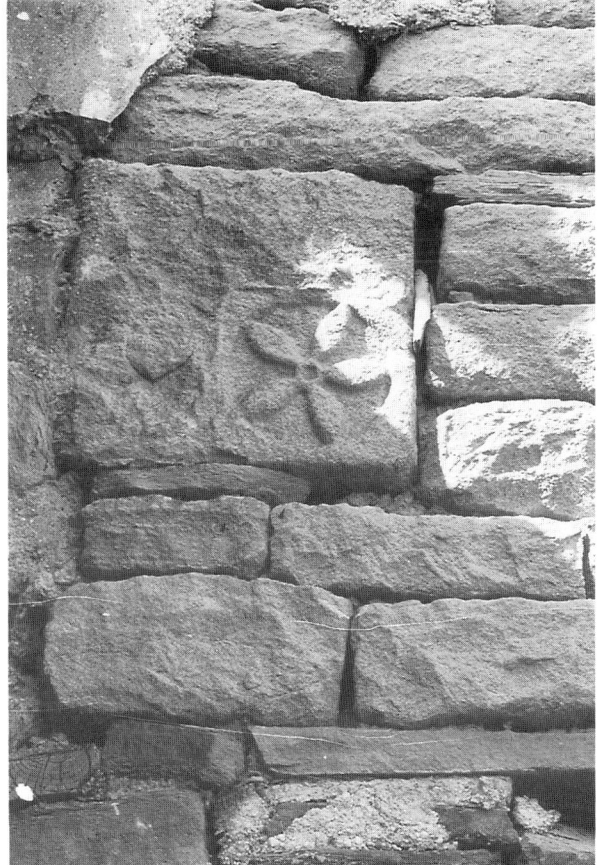

Decorative carving on a stone now in part of the rebuilt south gable. This may have been associated with a hood mould over a window on the west side.

clear but they may have been to light a boxed-in staircase.

The present fireplace in the south gable is late eighteenth century and the lintel is decorated by a central geometrical floral motif while the upper corners have quarter segments of the same motif. This decoration is found on a few early nineteenth century buildings in the area, usually on the door lintels.[34]

A stone with a floral design in high relief similar to the hood mould decoration at the Old Parsonage but smaller, is built into the masonry blocking a former doorway once leading through the south gable into the 1740's addition – the 'new chamber' and the 'Porch'.

The gable entrance plan is found in limited numbers throughout the British Isles. However in Saddleworth it is the most common position for an entrance into the housepart. Perhaps one reason could be the way in which many houses are sited along the valley sides using the narrow platforms with the ground rising behind and falling away in front, in which case an entrance along the platform would be the most feasible.

Number 2 Stonebreaks is one such example. It now forms the centre of a group of buildings, domestic and agricultural at Shaw Fold, Stonebreaks, but it once stood alone on a narrow platform. It is relatively small being twenty-six feet in length and twenty-three feet wide. It is a two-unit plan with features in common with the previous examples, viz. gable entrance, fireside window in addition to the housepart window, two windows to the pantry, etc., but the ground floor windows have hood moulds over them, those to the pantry at the rear being of flagstone projecting above the lintel but the windows to the housepart and parlour on the east front have well cut hood moulds with labels, those on the housepart terminating in square plaques on which are carved the initials 'J' and 'W' for James (or John) Winterbotham. These are the most elaborate hood moulds in Saddleworth and fit into the fashion of such ornamentation then being developed in west Yorkshire, over the watershed, in the later seventeenth century. This brings one to examine a door lintel on the house opposite known as the Parsonage. This lintel bears the initials and date 'JWJ 1687', but the lintel and door jambs are earlier than the building which has all the characteristics of the latter half of the eighteenth century, especially in the design and construction of the windows. At that time a small addition had been made to the old house at the north west corner so taking the original entrance into the new ground floor room. Possibly as a gesture to the thread of ownership the lintel could then have been moved to its present site.

The windows of the first floor of number 2 are of a later construction and may relate to a heightening of the building possibly at the same time as the small northerly extension.

Hood moulds are rare in Saddleworth and not all buildings contemporary with each other necessarily had them, in fact the majority were without. So there never was a tradition of using hood moulds, it was more a matter of fashion and therefore says something about the builders who were using them as symbols of status, especially so with the example described above.

At Ralph's, Denshaw, only the left-hand of the two two-light pantry windows has a hood mould; the significance of this is not yet clear. A date of 1675 (?) appears on the east gable on a re-used door lintel now placed upside down and acting as a window sill. At New Tame, between Delph and Denshaw, there still remains a six-light window with chamfered mullions and a good hood mould with upturned terminals. This window would appear to date from the 1680's. The same type of hood mould is still to be seen at number 54 Oldham Road, Grasscroft, over the housepart window and the former parlour window. An old photograph clearly shows a two-light fireside window to the left of the housepart window also with the same hood mould and these two are linked.[35] The walls are now rendered making investigation very difficult but the external evidence mentioned above

Number 2 Stonebreaks from the south-east.

Number 2 Stonebreaks from the south-west. Note the two-light pantry window at the rear.

Number 2 Stonebreaks. Detail of windows to the housepart and the hood mould with the initials 'J' and 'W' on the label stops.

New Tame. Six-light window with chamfered mullions, hood mould and hood mould stops.

56 Oldham Road, Grasscroft. The hood moulds are original, but the windows have been lowered.

Photograph of the Farrars Arms circa 1900. Note the arrangement of windows at number 54 Oldham Road which is on the extreme right.

would suggest that in this range of buildings is a small late seventeenth century Saddleworth type of house, extended eastwards to include a rear wing in the mid-eighteenth century. This is the building that George Shaw includes in his drawing which attempted to recreate Shaw Hall where it is shown as the small wing at the right-hand end of the building.

The only other known example in Saddleworth of this type of hood mould is at Pinfold on Knowl Top Lane, Greenfield. This is over the housepart window of four-lights with cavetto section mullions on the entrance front. The former three-light window plus a two-light fireside window at the rear of the housepart never had a hood mould so it is clear that such a feature was symbolic of status through decoration. At Pinfold the entrance is in a similar position to those at Windy Nook and Bank Top, opposite to the spere of the inglenook but the window hood mould places this part of the building in the later seventeenth century, perhaps in the time of Edmund Buckley whose daughter Ann was born in 1662. Two years later he paid Hearth Tax on one hearth. Only the housepart now remains from this period and the general dimensions are a little larger than those of the buildings described above, all are twenty-three feet wide but Pinfold is twenty-three feet long, whereas Stonebreaks is nineteen feet, Bank Top eighteen feet and Windy Nook seventeen feet long respectively.

Pinfold differs from the other buildings so far described in the scale of the masonry used in the walling of the late seventeenth century portion. Some coursing is up to fifteen inches high with the stones being proportionally long. The quality of workmanship is high – the joints are still fine and the nibs (corner edges) of the stones still sharp showing little sign of weathering. Pinfold stands in an exposed position on the shallower slopes of the east side of the Tame Valley and provides excellent testimony to the qualities of the local building stone. No doubt the larger facing stones had the advantage of needing fewer joints in the masonry and so restricting possible rain penetration.

The use of large coursing is also found at Furlane Cottage in Greenfield. As with Pinfold all that remains of the earlier building on the site is the housepart, clearly identified by the two-light fireside window and five-light housepart window which have cavetto mullions but no hood moulds. At the rear (west) is an inserted modern window and above that a four-light window with similar details. This window is in its original position and is a good guide to the former standard of accommodation on the upper floor, in this case with quite generous lights in the window, it would have been comfortable and well lit. The original entrance was in the south gable – now hidden by later building – leading into a housepart measuring twenty-two feet long by twenty-one feet wide.

In many Saddleworth houses which have been altered and enlarged it is often the housepart that has survived complete, the parlour or pantry bay being rebuilt or totally replaced. At Pinfold the original parlour was replaced in the early eighteenth century by an extension including an elegant three-light mullion window. At Fur Lane Cottage the parlour was replaced at the end of the eighteenth century, and it is worth recording that a floor joist in this newer bay has a series of angled half-lap joints for bracing and appears to have been a purlin, possibly from a cruck-framed building on this site. Similar examples of the housepart alone remaining are to be found at 8 Harrop Green and Rose Cottage, Tunstead.

A more complete Saddleworth house is number 2 Saddleworth Fold, built in 1699 by Joshua Radcliffe. This too was entered via the gable end but later extensions changed that and the datestone was replaced to a position over the housepart window. The original height of the walls is clearly discernable by a change in the coursing which occurred when the upper rooms were given higher ceilings round about 1800. A new range of windows was also included in this phase but the three-light window over the parlour still retained its original mullions though these were heightened by additional pieces.

Pinfold. Window to the housepart. Note the hood mould. Two mullions have been removed, the indication of their former position can be seen on the sill.

Pinfold. Rear view, the early windows are on the extreme left ground floor.

Pinfold. The east elevation showing the varied coursing of the walls, the result of many changes to the building.

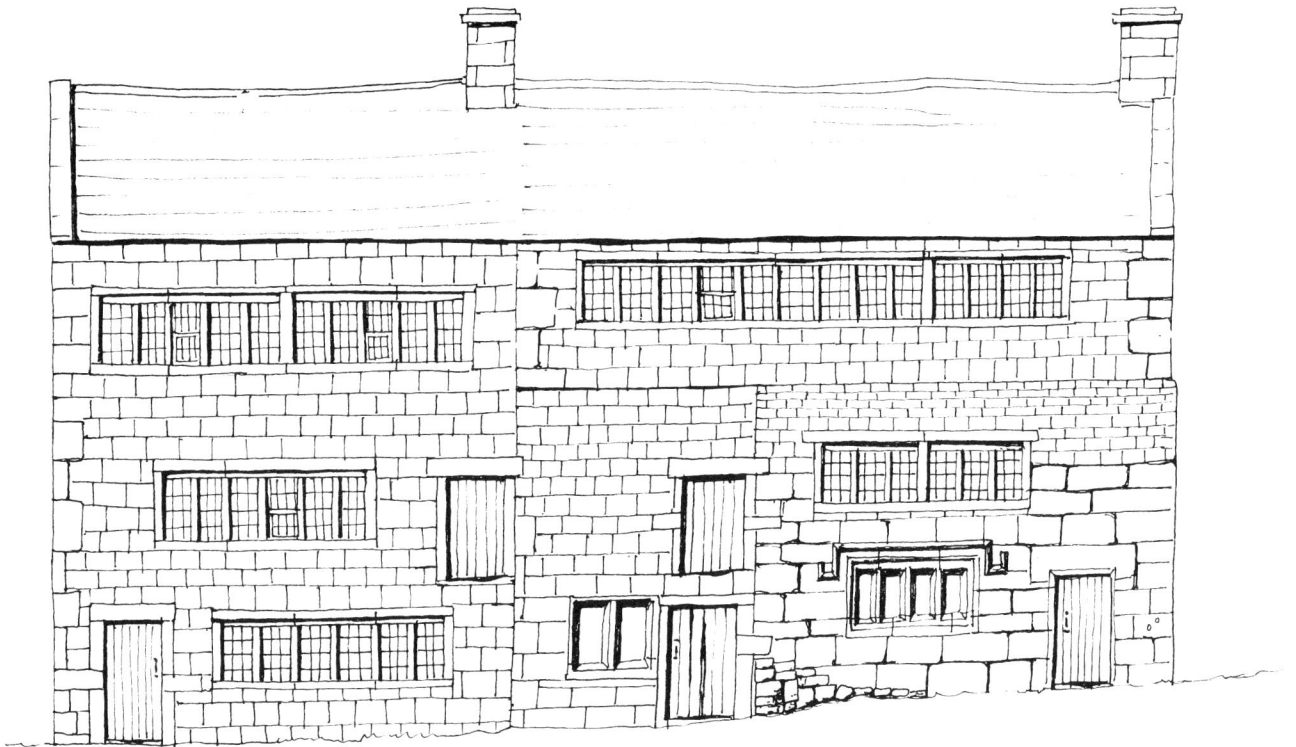

Pinfold. West elevation. In the drawing a later outshut has been omitted and the coursing of the walls emphasised.

Fur Lane Cottage, Greenfield. General view from the north.

Fur Lane Cottage, Greenfield. Housepart window and fireside window of the earlier building.

Fur Lane Cottage, Greenfield. General view from the west side. Note the four-light mullion window of the earlier building.

Number 2 Saddleworth Fold. View from the west.

Number 2 Saddleworth Fold. Housepart window with the original door lintel repositioned above.

Woolleys, Greenfield. View from the south.

Woolleys, Greenfield. View from the north showing the small square staircase window and two-light pantry window.

Woolleys on Friezeland Lane, Greenfield is a good surviving example of a Saddleworth house, undated but built circa 1720. Described as a 'dwelling House with 2 Bays but with indifferent Outhousing' in 1770, the 'indifferent Outhousing' has long since gone but John Woolley's home remains,[36] with some additional windows and the east gable entrance having been rebuilt. A small square window set mid-height on the north side indicates the position of the staircase which would have been boxed in, hence the need for light. The only other window on this side is a two-light mullion window lighting the pantry which had until recently a stone shelf set against the two outer walls. The parlour was entered through the pantry, an arrangement common in Saddleworth as was the provision of the staircase within the pantry area. The present central fireplace and chimney stack is quite recent and it is probable that the partition between the housepart and unheated parlour was originally of timber-framed construction.

A subtle change marks Woolleys and number 2 Saddleworth Fold from the other examples described and mentioned, this is in the relationship between the windows of the housepart and fireside window. Whereas in the earlier buildings the lintel of the fireside window had been some nine inches lower than that of the housepart, in the above two buildings – and later ones – they are of the same height which helps to create a greater sense of unity in the design of the main front, thus leading to a conscious sense of design in the Saddleworth house as the eighteenth century opens.

The buildings discussed so far represent the achievement in building reached in Saddleworth by the end of the seventeenth century. The houses are well built structures planned for a simple life and giving shelter to a population which had to endure a harsh climate and a limited agrarian economy. The poor nature of the soil, the topography and wet climate limited farming to a predominantly pastoral economy, the fields yielding a few arable crops and a hay harvest but being mainly used for grazing cattle and sheep. The farms were not large but all too often fields and pastures were some distance away from each other – a result of the partible inheritance system whereby property was divided at death between all the children. The effect of this system was that land was continually being subdivided among an ever increasing population until the individual holdings became too small to support their occupants by agriculture alone.

Unfortunately manorial records are not available for this period and wills and inventories supply personal details for a very small percentage of the population at any one time, so in order to gain some sort of picture of the social structure in Saddleworth at the close of the seventeenth century the Hearth Tax Returns have been used.[37] These Returns exist for 1664, 1666, 1669–70 and 1672, and for the purpose of this study the Returns for 1664 have been used. They encompass everyone and were not concerned with who was a freeholder or tenant so the whole of the population of Saddleworth was included.

The total number of households in Saddleworth considered for tax is 286 which includes those householders not chargeable for tax who numbered 78. One householder payed for 5 hearths, this was James Kenworthy, Senior, but it is not made clear whether these five hearths were in the same house or a house and cottages. Two houses had 4 hearths, Peter Bradbury of Peters and Thomas Whitehead; 8 had three hearths and 16 two hearths. the remaining 181 had one hearth and presumably those exempt from paying tax would have had one fireplace but their circumstances made them as 'non chargeable', i.e. too poor to pay.

So it can be presumed that 259 houses in Saddleworth were classed as having one hearth per house. A poor community? Not necessarily so in view of the quality of the buildings featured above and which had only one hearth each. But it must also be realised that there would have been many Saddleworthians still living in the more primitive types of shelter mentioned in an earlier section. The large percentage of single hearths also points to a relatively unstratified society, perhaps quietly wealthy rather than deprived.

From the number of houses given in the Hearth Tax Return for 1664, and using Joan Thursk's multiplier,[38] with a generous allowance for multiple occupation, sub-letting and evasion, a population in the region of 2000 for Saddleworth can be estimated for this date. Compared with the Protestation Returns of 1642[39] which list 384 adult males, producing an estimated population of 1600, the degree of population increase can be appreciated.

The increasing number of substantial stone houses that begin to appear in Saddleworth from the late seventeenth century suggests a rising economy that was the result of agriculture plus a second means of income; the former occupation gave subsistence while the second provided for some economic growth in the area. This was the phenomenon of the dual economy which in the case of Saddleworth and the Pennine region was the production in the home of textiles – mainly woollen cloth.

Several factors encouraged the development of textile production in the Pennines from the late sixteenth century. First, the area was too remote for a textile industry to be dominated by a craft guild; there was the need to redress the balance of agricultural income-loss due to the practice of partible inheritance; a pastoral economy gave the inhabitants time to follow other occupations some of which would have taken the form of a service industry such as a mason, carpenter, tailor or shoemaker for instance. Finally, to set up as a clothier was relatively easy, the equipment and method of production did not yet require specialist accommodation, the looms were small and the spinning wheels very portable. The equipment was inexpensive, a pair of looms was worth 10 shillings and spinning wheels between 2 and 4 shillings in the late seventeenth century. Compare these figures with the value of livestock at the same period, 18 shillings for a pig and £2. 2s. 0d. for a cow. The family could provide the workforce and there also began a system of middlemen, who supplied the raw material and who would market the end product. The area had natural advantages too, particularly an abundance of soft water for washing the wool and woollen cloth and also providing a source of power for fulling mills. As the production of textiles developed the network of packhorse tracks expanded.

The Process of Making Woollen Cloth in Saddleworth

The process of making woollen cloth had been perfected over many centuries and was well suited to a domestic situation as no elaborate machines were required. The first stage was the preparation of the fleece, removing the burrs, dried dirt and natural fats deposited in the wool. To remove the natural oils the wool was washed in lye, a solution of water and amonia, the latter usually collected in the form of animal or human urine (lant). A novel method of quickly drying the washed wool was well established in the Pennines by the end of the seventeenth century, it was called 'wuzzing'. It was simplicity itself, a pole a yard long was set in a convenient hole on a house or wall (wuzzing hole) and an open weave basket suspended from a ring encircling the pole which then allowed the basket to swing freely when the pole was rapidly rotated at the free end. It was the forerunner of the spin dryer, very efficient and costing only the labour. There are wuzzing holes in abundance in Saddleworth, some set very low, however one must not presume that small children were employed, but rather that the present ground level has risen. The 'wool wall' at Beswick's on Grains Road, Delph, may have provided an alternative method of drying the washed fleece.[40] The remaining foreign matter such as seeds was now removed by hand, a job for small fingers. Blending could then be carried out, mixing wool from various fleeces for colour and texture. In this process oil or fat was added prior to carding, to help the wool open out and allow the tangled fleece to slip apart. The inventory of Edmund Buckley

Knott Hill, Delph. Wuzzing holes by the barn door.

The 'wool wall' at Beswick's, Delph.

of Lydiate (1718) lists,

'Item in Woole yarne, Oyle and dingstuffe (dying stuff) . . . £25. 15s. 0d.' [41]

Rancid butter was frequently used as the 'oyle', this lubricant would also lessen the amount of wool dust and fluff in the atmosphere of the working place.

The next stage was very important and determined the quality of the finished cloth. This was carding which opened out the tangled fleece and made the rovings for spinning. Cards were made of metal staples set in a piece of leather mounted on a wooden board with a handle on it. The staples were springy and sloped uniformly in one direction so that the staples on the two cards could pull at the fleece, straighten tangles and spread the wool evenly over the surface; this was then gathered into a roving. Edmund Buckley's inventory mentions one 'Paire of . . . combs' for these were operated in pairs, one gripping the fleece while the other combed and pulled the wool fibres into order. The roving – or sliver – was then ready for the spinner.

In some Pennine areas homesteads tended to specialise in either spinning or weaving, this was particularly the case around Halifax, but in Saddleworth both processes were often carried out in the same place. Inventories frequently list wheels and looms together amongst the household goods indicating that the Saddleworth clothier had control over all the basic processes of making cloth; the carding, spinning and weaving being done within his house. The family would no doubt be employed but journeymen – those who worked by the day – might also be employed. The Will of Edmund Buckley of Lydiate is helpful on this point; he gives to his younger son Robert,

'. . . that paire of loomes which he or his man usually weave in . . .'.

The looms being thus disposed of in the Will they are not then listed in the inventory.

Because woollen broadcloth and not worsteds were made in Saddleworth, spinning was the simple operation of drawing out the rovings and putting in a twist to give strength and uniformity to the yarn. The 'great wheel' commonly used in Saddleworth was a large wooden-spoked wheel eighteen to twenty-four inches in diameter giving direct drive to a spindle by means of a cord belt, the whole arranged in a simple wooden frame. The wheel had to be turned by hand and the gearing was such that the spindle revolved at a high speed. 'Wheels' appear frequently in inventories and are valued cheaply, around 2 shillings. It is unlikely that the more elaborate Saxony spinning wheel with flyers was used and as these wheels are more like pieces of furniture with turned legs and supports plus a treadle mechanism to turn the wheel, their value given in inventories would have been much greater than 2 shillings.

The spun yarn was then prepared for use as warp or weft. The warp was made by passing the yarn round widely spaced pegs set in a wall, or on a warping frame, adjusted to the length required. Edmund Buckley's inventory of 1718 lists a 'warping wall'. To give the yarn of the warp some added strength to withstand the friction of passing through the loom it was given a coating of size, usually a vegetable starch plus alum. In some areas this was done by dipping the warp into a size solution. In the mid-Pennines sizing often took place out of doors; the warp was stretched along a series of horizontal supports, size was applied and dried with the help of the breeze. Places where this was done were called 'stretcher gates',[42] two good examples are to be seen near Cowpe in Rossendale and another at Mount Tabor near Luddenden. Both are on local trackways so the weavers avoided trespassing on farmland. At Mount Tabor the walled track doubles in width to accommodate a series of low vertical stones placed at regular intervals.

The warps were supported on poles which were placed between these stones and the field wall. Another stretcher gate can be found near Holme, south of Holmfirth, this used an elevated bank by the east side of the former trackway, now a minor road. Stones forming the capping to this wall show evidence of having once supported square, wooden poles, reaching out horizontally on both sides of the wall. From these examples it is possible to try and identify stretcher gates in Saddleworth, and two sections on Long Lane between Tunstead and Binn Green seem to be likely sites.

The sized warp was taken and wound onto the warp beam (or roller) on the loom, each thread was then drawn through a heddle a large number of which were suspended in a heald of which there were at least two, in order to make a 'shed'. The shuttle carrying the weft was passed by hand through the shed. The warp then passed through a reed which helped to maintain the width of the cloth and also to beat up each weft thread passed through the shed by the shuttle, close to the previously thrown weft. The warp was then tied on to the end beam which would then take up the woven cloth. The looms were simple in construction and were made to be easily dismantled in order that they could be moved from room to room or to another place altogether. The final stages in making woollen cloth took place in mills. The cloth was dyed and then fulled, scoured to remove the soap from fulling and then dried and stretched on tenters. Finally the woollen cloth would be cropped to give it a uniformly smooth surface and make it ready for market. The whole process was technically simple but considerable skill was needed to produce good quality cloth capable of lasting through more than one generation without wearing out.

There was little need for large specialist accommodation for cloth-making since the warping frames, spinning wheels and looms took up little space and were relatively portable; spinning could be done out of doors in suitable weather. Inventories relating to Saddleworth during this period make it clear that looms and wheels were to be found in the housepart, parlour or chambers and occasionally in 'the shop'. The long 'weavers lights' were not to appear until much later, after 1770.

The raw material for the woollen industry could come from as far away as Shropshire in addition to the wool from sheep bred and reared locally.[43] This was to produce the varieties of texture and colour of the cloth made in Saddleworth, the 'broads' and 'narrows' and the kerseymeres, honleys, elastics and beaverettes, cloths for which Saddleworth became famous during the eighteenth century. In contrast to this worsteds were made from the longer wool of sheep reared in east Yorkshire and in Lincolnshire, much nearer to hand.

The number of houses surviving from the seventeenth century is small; it appears that these houses were the homes of the more wealthy members of the community, yet they come nowhere near the ostentation of contemporary houses being built during this period around Halifax and Rochdale.[44]

A stretcher gate above Cowpe, Rossendale.

Numbers 9 and 11 Clough Lane, Grasscroft. The original building extended as far as the remaining quoin stone seen below the left-hand chimney stack.

Chapter 4.   Eighteenth Century Developments

The degree of sophistication in the design of Saddleworth houses reached higher levels in the eighteenth century. The basic plan-form underwent some modification. At Tunstead, Grasscroft and Gatehead there are two-bay houses but with an additional room alongside the housepart thus making an 'L' shaped plan. Some are of two floors while others may have been single storeyed. This extra room or rooms could have provided additional space for the secondary source of income. In the inventory of Nathaniel Holden of Kinders, 1745, there is a mention of a 'loomhouse' adjoining the parlour; the term 'shop' is also used to mean a workshop as in the inventory of Robert Mayall of Shelderslow, 1721.[45]

Numbers 9 to 11 Clough Lane, Grasscroft, once a single building, is a good example of an early eighteenth century house with a loomshop or dairy behind the housepart which is entered by a gable entrance. The main body of the house is a typical Saddleworth two-bay plan with, on the south front, the fireside, housepart and parlour windows all of the same height. At the rear is the two-storey wing with a six-light mullion window on the first floor to give light to a large chamber which also had a small fireplace on the north wall. These two features were to become very much associated with the domestic system of textile production later in the century. The ground floor room has a four-light window but of a later period suggesting that it replaced a smaller window, perhaps of a dairy, the north side of a house being a good position for such a room. The staircase was in the housepart and access to the loomshop was via the chamber over the housepart.

Before alteration in the 1970's Lower Tunstead was a good example of a house built with an outshut to the rear. The entrance into this house was via the west gable direct into the housepart; to the left is the small room seventeen feet by seven with a small three-light window to the north. From the evidence of the masonry of the west gable (before it was covered by the later addition) this was originally a ground floor room only with a lean-to roof and of the same early eighteenth century build as the rest of the house, and may have been the dairy or buttery. This would have enabled the parlour to occupy the full width of the building; it should be noted that there were no windows originally in the north wall of this end bay.

Lower Tunstead also shows another change in tradition. In the housepart the wall normally found between the fireside window and that of the housepart is here reduced to being a king mullion, a mullion extending the full depth of the wall and correspondingly wider than a standard mullion. This would suggest that the tradition of having a distinctive inglenook was disappearing, but that the separate window for the fireplace survived.

The most distinctive and important feature to note here is the masonry. In the best local tradition gritstone is used for the quoins, door and window details, and the walls built in diminishing courses of gritstone. But at Tunstead instead of the walls presenting a flush face, the outer face of each course is set at a slight angle to the vertical, the upper edge projecting beyond the lower edge by up to an inch. Seen in profile this gives the wall a saw tooth effect. This is water-shot coursing. The technique is known by various names in the Pennines, 'ramped' in Rochdale, 'overshot' in Darwin, 'T masonry' in Rossendale, 'weathershot' in North Yorkshire and 'Yorkshire tilt' in Saddleworth. First used in rural areas in the late seventeenth century, the practice of building water-shot walls became widespread throughout the Pennine region during the next hundred and fifty years.

As the practice swiftly became widespread there must have been a good reason for it; but how and when the technique originated in the Pennines is not yet clear. The earliest example so far identified is at Mereclough, Cliviger, in a small building dated 1670. Published references are few and there is no mention of the technique in eighteenth or nineteenth century building manuals. This is not perhaps surprising as they are usually

Numbers 9 and 11 Clough Lane, Grasscroft. The original entrance is now a window. Note the difference between the mullions of both sets of windows.

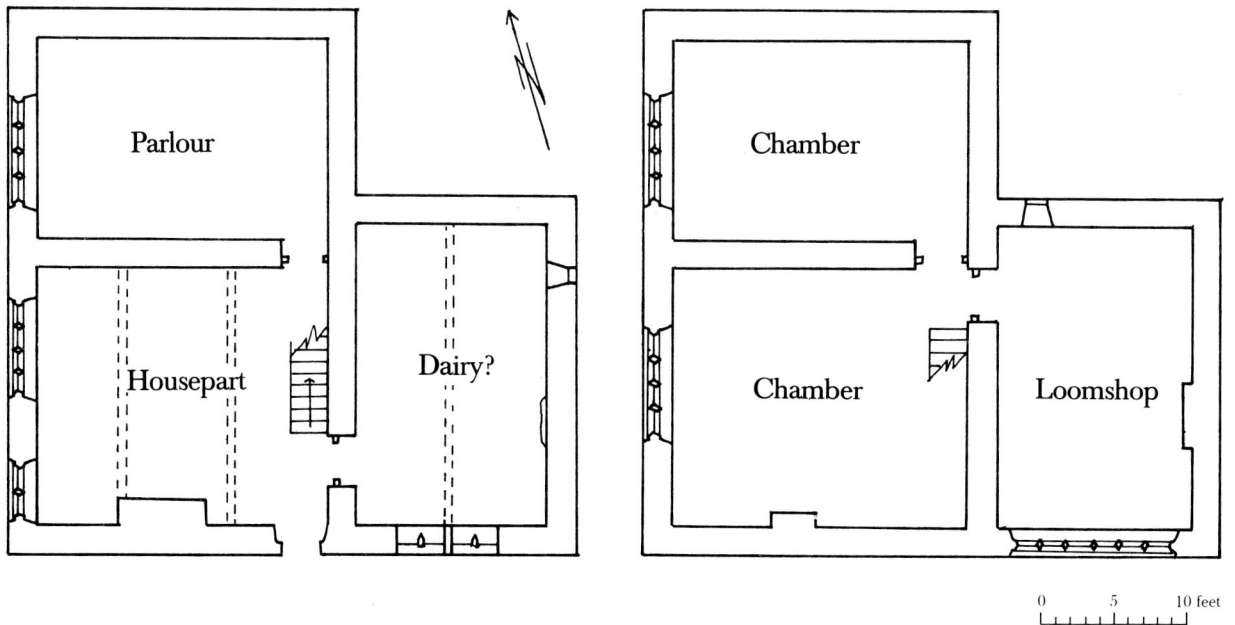

Numbers 9–11 Clough Lane, Grasscroft. Plans of ground and first floors.

Lower Tunstead. The extent of the original building is indicated by the quoins still in situ. The former two-light fireside window has been made into an entrance door.

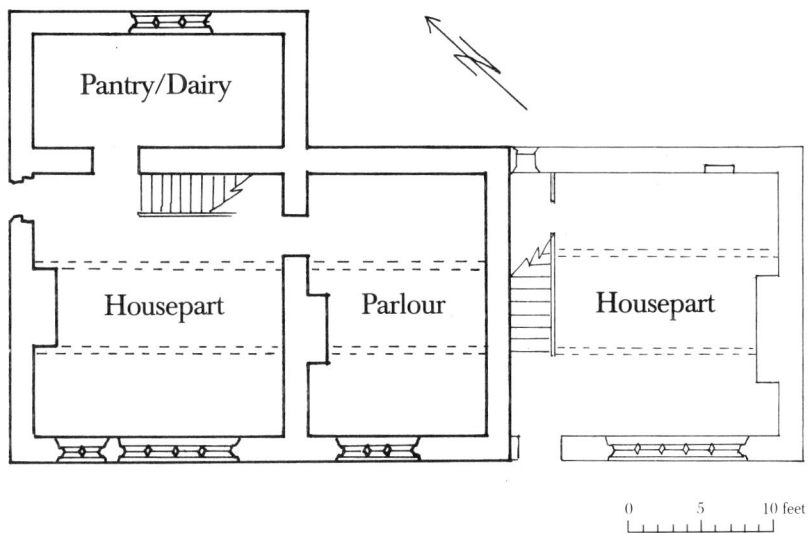

Lower Tunstead. Ground floor plan before alterations.

Water-shot coursing at Edge End, Greenfield.
Note how the tilt is achieved over the window
jamb, by using a small stone under the
through stone.

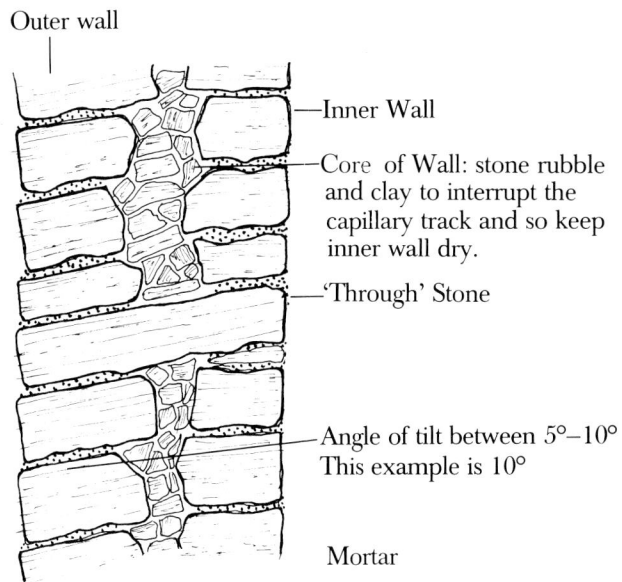

Outer wall

Inner Wall

Core of Wall: stone rubble
and clay to interrupt the
capillary track and so keep
inner wall dry.

'Through' Stone

Angle of tilt between 5°–10°
This example is 10°

Mortar

Water-shot coursing. Diagram showing a typical cross-section.

more concerned with 'polite' buildings than vernacular techniques.[46]

Water-shot coursing appears to have been first recognised by W. B. McKay in 1938,[47] when he identified it as a typical central Lake District technique of walling where the local slate stone – impervious to water – was bedded to slope down to the outer face, which would have helped to prevent water penetration of the wall. If rain was blown into the wall joints it would run out. In the Pennines it is only the outer skin of the wall that is laid in this fashion – and the sandstone absorbs water. The joints between the walling stones are made very fine to prevent or limit water penetration into the soft mortar, but sandstone absorbs water by capillary action and to allow the water content to remain in the wall would lead to problems of damp and the deterioration of the walling stone. The downward tilt of the outer face stones would encourage the water to percolate to the outer ledge from which it would be removed by evaporation. The success of the technique is undeniable, for in some recent instances of renovations where the stone walls were rebuilt in flush wall masonry, damp has appeared when before there had been no such problem. With very few exceptions, all buildings described in the rest of this book have walls of water-shot coursing.

To return to the house at Lower Tunstead, similar examples of the small room adjoining the housepart are to be seen at Gatehead Farm and Lower Gatehead Cottage. Both were built by sons of Edmund Buckley of Lydiate who died in 1718. Gatehead Farm was completed by Robert Buckley, a clothier, who was left 'stone timber and boards' to the value of £18 in addition to the residue 'of my whole estate (which) I give to my son Robert Buckley towards the building and repairing of the housing at Gatehead'. The lintel over the gable entrance has the initials and date R B 1718. Edmund Buckley died in June 1718 and so it is probable that the house was completed by the end of that year. From the evidence of Old Bent House near Littleborough, built between March and September 1691, the main walls of the building could be raised within six weeks.[48] If it were possible to calculate what the 'residue' of Edmund Buckley's estate was it would be possible to estimate the cost of building Gatehead Farm.

Robert Buckley's occupation is given as a clothmaker when in the following year of 1719 his tenancy of the Gatehead property was confirmed for a term of 'Fourscore and Nineteen Yeares'.[49] His house too, had a small side wing on the north side of the gable entrance but this was of two storeys, perhaps an arrangement similar to that on Clough Lane, but here at Gatehead this wing has been partially rebuilt in the early nineteenth century.

Robert's brother, James Buckley, also described as a 'clothmaker', built a similar house a few yards to the west of Gatehead Farm in 1720. The datestone for this house is on the east gable and is a stone set diamond fashion and was inscribed with the initials and date J B 1720, but it has now eroded away.[50] This house also had a side wing but quite unlike any other in Saddleworth. To the left of the gable entrance and inset into the wall is a long deep lintel very similar to those found on barns of this period but this wing lacks the length and depth for a barn and on the first floor there is a large room with a five-light window facing west. The upper floor has been added at a much later date. Perhaps the ground floor was used for storing the sledges used by farmers to carry hay and other crops from their fields to the barn. There had been an old barn (described as such in 1770) just to the north of Gatehead Farm.

This type of Saddleworth house continued into the mid-eighteenth century with Oak Lea House, Church Fields, Dobcross, built in 1747 by John Harrop. The datestone to this house is particularly fine being skilfully cut with very decorative initials, with a fleur de lys and thistles as a central motif. Unfortunately, to achieve this fine detail the design was cut on the bed of a fine-grained sandstone which, when placed over the door, was laid

Water-shot coursing at Higher Cross. It is noticeable where the wall meets up with the middle window jamb.

Water-shot coursing at Higher Slack.

Gatehead Farm, Delph. The house completed by Robert Buckley in 1718. The gable entrance is hidden by the one-storey wing.

Gatehead Farm, Delph. Part of the side wing. Note the change in the masonry when this wing was enlarged in the early nineteenth century.

Lower Gatehead Cottage, Delph. Built by James Buckley in 1720. The side wing. The lintel of the barn (?) door is clearly visible. The small two-light window at the eaves shows where the wing was heightened.

Oak Lea House, Dobcross. The lintel over the original gable entrance.

Oak Lea House, Dobcross. View from Church Fields.

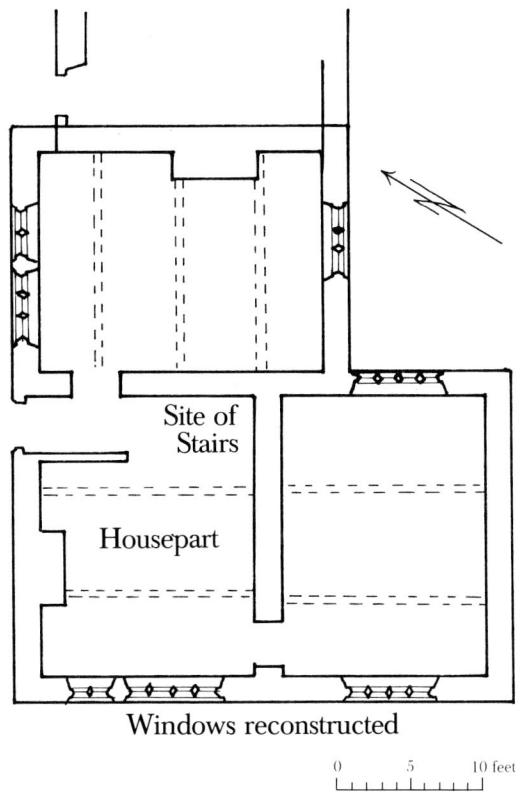

Oak Lea House, Dobcross. Ground floor plan of the house as built.

Site of
Stairs

Housepart

Windows reconstructed

0   5   10 feet

Oakdene Cottage, Deanhead. Originally two cottages built shortly after 1742.

with the bed in the vertical plane and the weather is gradually splitting the carved surface from the rest of the lintel.

This lintel is set over the original entrance to the house in the north gable, and to the left is the one room two-storey wing of the same build. This is a large wing with a generous number of windows in the north and south walls; the ground floor has a five-light window with a king mullion on the north side which gives the impression that here is a two-light fireside window plus the three-light housepart window (as at Lower Tunstead). In the east gable is a fireplace, the stone stack of which is shared by number 6 Church Fields adjoining. The ground floor rooms are all fairly equal in size with the parlour originally being unheated.

The west front had alterations carried out in the early nineteenth century when the mullion windows on the ground floor were replaced by double Georgian sash windows and a new central doorway added. A classical moulded cornice was also added to the eaves of what then became the main front. Appropriate changes were made internally.

An arrangement of cottages unusual in Saddleworth is to be found at Deanhead. Now known as Oakdene, this was formerly two cottages one the identical mirror image of the other, both having gable entrances and both originally having a smoke hood. They were built by the Rhodes family some time after 1742 and fifty years later were very much altered.[51] This change is described later. A similar pair has been recorded at 32 and 33 Oldfield, Honley near Huddersfield, where the datestone reads 1742.[52] In this particular case this date is doubtful for the building has all the characteristics of the very late eighteenth century from the details of doorway construction, proportion of the ground floor windows and use of square set mullions. The datestone now over the two adjoining doors was most probably from an earlier building on the site. But there is no doubt about the original plan and appearance of Oakdene Cottage nor of its date.

Another 'dual' house is the 'Cross Keys', above Saddleworth Fold and on the line of an old packhorse track. The Cross Keys may always have been an inn since it was built in 1745 and if this is the case it may explain its unique arrangement of rooms.[53] The main front is to the south east and the arrangement of windows and doors clearly shows two houses. The main door has the inscribed lintel MB SB 1745 and is decorated by a half-roll moulding running under the lintel and down each door jamb to within eight inches of the ground. This degree of decoration is unusual in Saddleworth and here at the Cross Keys there are two more similar doorways but without initials or dates. The second doorway is further along the front to the north and is now a window but the jambs of the doorway can be clearly seen with the half-roll moulding. What is now a door at that end of the building was originally a two-light window similar to that remaining to the right of the door. This end of the building may well have been a house or cottage independent of the inn.

At the rear the ground falls away sharply and this has enabled a basement storey to be built beneath the inn. Here is another door with the same detailing as the other two and again partially blocked to make a window. The internal arrangements have changed in recent times and an additional bay of building has been added to the rear, but the building must always have been imposing as befitted an important hostelry on the main north–south route through Saddleworth. Another pair of dual houses is 23a and 25 King Street, Delph, built in 1769.

John Hegginbottom became incumbent of St. Chads, Saddleworth in 1721 and from this time the Parish Registers begin to contain much information of value to the history of Saddleworth. The entries are very detailed giving the name of both parents in the case of a baptism plus the occupation of the father and where he lived, and the marriage and burial entries are equally informative. M. T. Wild has made a study of the Registers from 1721–1791 and from his tables it is clear how far Saddleworth had become committed to textile production by that period.[54] In the five years from 1722 to 1726, 75.6% of the

Cross Keys Inn. General view. The old track runs along the front of the building.

Cross Keys Inn. The second door now blocked to make a window.

Cross Keys Inn. Date stone over the main entrance.

Cross Keys, Inn. Rear view.

Cross Keys Inn. Rear door.

Numbers 23a and 25 King Street, Delph. Pair of cottages built in 1769.

male population were involved in textiles and only 11.4% recorded as yeomen or husbandmen. Fifty years later, in the period 1770 to 1774 the percentages had changed, that of males in textiles increasing to 89.2% while those in husbandry had fallen to a mere 3.1%.

Most of those involved in textiles were recorded as 'clothiers', a term which would indicate that they considered themselves to be a superior class of cloth manufacturer, involved in the production of cloth from the raw material to the product ready for market. These clothiers rarely employed persons from outside their own families. This was in contrast to adjoining regions, such as the worsted area around Halifax, where the 'putting-out' system was in use. There the raw material was distributed to the spinners and then the yarn taken to an employee class of handloom weavers to be woven up.

This degree of independence of the clothiers of Saddleworth is reflected in their homes. Some properties were freehold, notably in Friarmere and parts of Quickmere and those living within the Manor of Saddleworth were able to negotiate reasonable leases from the Manor. Whether freehold or leasehold there is no obvious distinction between the houses in the mid-eighteenth century.

It comes as no surprise that one of the earliest buildings to show a marked change from the established pattern was built by a Buckley. In 1717 Robert Buckley son of John Buckley of Overhouse in Grasscroft, and a wealthy yeoman, built a house on land he had inherited in 1710.[55] Now known as 16b Clough Lane, Buckley's house showed a marked change from those to be built by his kinsmen at Gatehead in 1718 and 1720. Robert Buckley's house is entered from the front of the building through a doorway left of centre. Although not fully achieved there is an obvious attempt at a symmetrical façade, though a more conventional plan behind the front, prevented a central entrance. Instead the central feature is a pair of two-light windows, one above the other. Today these light a fine dog-leg staircase with turned balusters. However, this may not originally have been there; the landing on the stairs is nine inches above the window sill and this gap has been filled in in a makeshift manner, though what alternative use this narrow space could have had is difficult to decide. Prior to recent internal changes this staircase was set further back in the house, but it could have been moved there at an earlier period to be later put back in its original position. It is to be noted that the lack of planning co-ordination between staircase landings and window sills, and transomes, is more often the rule than the exception at this period.[56] Such a staircase must have been an innovation in Saddleworth where the simple ladder stair was the usual type, set against a rear or side wall and with the bottom of the stairs facing the entrance into the house. In many houses lying partly ruinous the position of the staircase can be seen from the impression of the wall string on the wall plaster, such as at Edge End below Pots and Pans, and formerly at Boothstead near Denshaw.

On the front elevation of Robert Buckley's house the windows to the rooms are all of three lights with cavetto mullions (except where these have been replaced during recent repairs), recessed but with no hood mould or string course. Until the addition of the cornice about 1800, the house would have presented a plain but dignified appearance and quite unlike any other in Saddleworth.

Another house in Saddleworth from this time, also allows the staircase to declare its position from the outside but otherwise is quite traditional. This is Thornlee Fold in Grotton, now ruinous. A two-light window is to the left of the three-light parlour window, but set a little higher; this was to fit the landing of a corner staircase which may have been enclosed by a framed partition hence the need for a window at landing level. From the area available for a staircase, which is limited, this stair must have been steep turning through 90 degrees at the landing. One advantage of this type of staircase was the smaller

Number 16b Clough Lane, Grasscroft. Elevation of the house built by Robert Buckley in 1717. The moulded cornice was added at the turn of the nineteenth century.

Number 16b Clough Lane, Grasscroft. View from the south-west.

Thornlee Fold, Grotton. The three-light window of the parlour has been broken through for a doorway. To the left is the two-light staircase window.

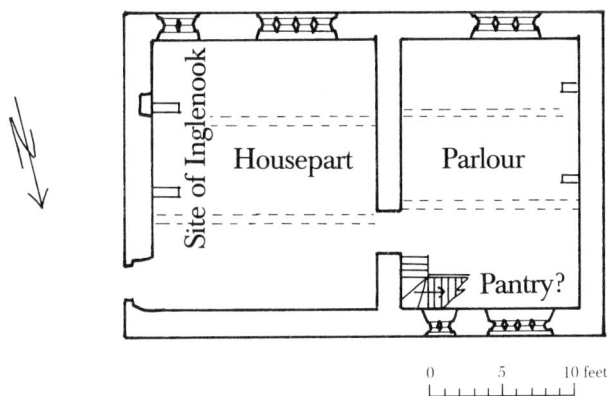

Thornlee Fold, Grotton. Ground floor plan.

area needed for a stairwell in the room above.

At the rear of Edgehill (originally known as Lower Barn) built in 1737, is a small one-light window set slightly higher than its two-light neighbour to the pantry; this too is to light a former enclosed staircase similar to one still surviving in Knowl Farm on Knowl Top Lane.[57]

Edgehill was built as a laithehouse, that is a building comprising a house, barn and byre all under one roof but without any inner communication or means of access between the house and laithe (barn and byre).[58] In this way the laithehouse differed from the longhouse which had been the basic rural house type from the sixth century to the fifteenth century by which time cattle were separately housed in barns or byres built away from the house across a farmyard. Only in very remote areas like West Wales, Dartmoor and the Hebrides was the longhouse tradition continued into recent times. The laithehouse was most suitable for mixed farming with a barn for storage of hay and corn and a byre for milking the cattle.

Before recent changes at the laithe end, Edgehill was fully recorded and the following description relates to the building as it existed before 1980. The present entrance is part of the late eighteenth century extension added to provide a large loomshop on the east end, and the original entrance in the east gable became an internal doorway. The lintel over this door records the initials of John and Margaret Buckley and the date 1737, presumably when the house was built. From the south front the housepart is recognised by the two-light fireside window and four-light housepart window. To the west a three-light window indicates the parlour originally entered from the pantry via the housepart. The windows to this pantry have been referred to above. All the windows have cavetto section mullions.

To the west follows the barn and byre, the former once having had a low barn door with a deep lintel. When this lintel was being removed recently, a stone relieving arch was discovered behind it which dispensed with the usual practice of using wooden lintels spanning the opening behind the stone lintel. Facing the barn door in the rear wall is a small door which is the threshing door, allowing the control of the draught across the threshing floor when winnowing. The low barn door restricted its use for waggons, but these were rarely used in farming in the central Pennines, instead large low horse-drawn sledges were used, the long runners making it easier to traverse the uneven and sometimes stony ground. On the steeply sloping fields the lower centre of gravity of a sledge gave greater stability to a load of hay or corn. In the inventory of Joseph Schofield of Arthurs in Greenfield, a clothier, dated November 1712, are listed four sledges used to bring in 'corne and hay', valued at £4.[59] There are many examples of barns with similar barn doors; at Hollins Farm, another laithehouse on the Holmfirth Road, Greenfield, at the barn added to Bank Top in the mid-eighteenth century, and at Briarfield Cottage on Sandy Lane, Dobcross. At Edgehill a byre at the west end completed the complex. This would have been used as a milking parlour, perhaps with some cattle being sheltered there in the more severe winter weather.

Edgehill is the earliest dated laithehouse in Saddleworth. Some years later Delph Slack was built by Robert Whitehead whose initials together with that of his wife Anne and the date 1745, appear on the lintel over the east gable entrance. Like Edgehill, this is a laithehouse later extended, but in this case at both ends. At the east end a dairy was added and the byre extended to the west. In spite of later alterations – the subdivision of the barn and introduction of new windows – the original south façade is still clear. The original windows are still made from millstone grit cut to the cavetto section and the walling being of narrow flags with gritstone quoins. However, the three-light parlour window has lost its mullions and the sill has been lowered and similar changes have happened to the window

Threshing Door

Byre

Barn

Pantry

Parlour

Houspart

0   5   10 feet

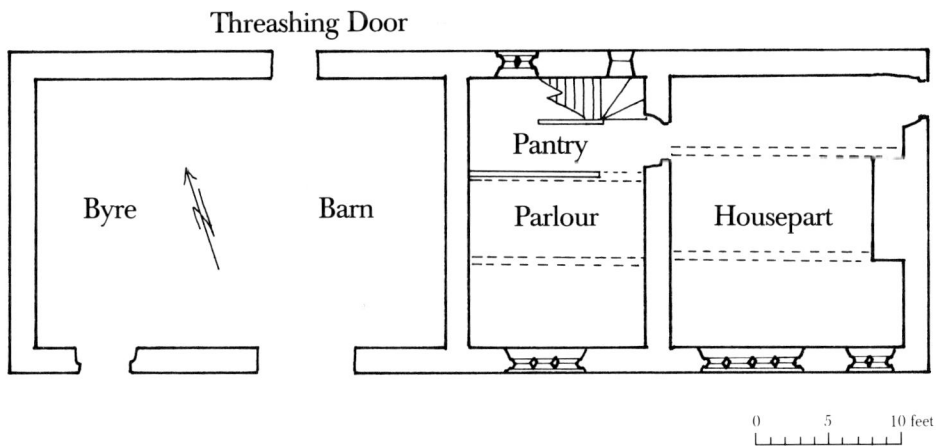

Edge Hill, Delph. Elevation and ground floor plan of the building as built in 1737.

Edge Hill, Delph. View from the south. The nearer bay was added to the 1737 building at the turn of the nineteenth century.

Edge Hill, Delph. The former barn door.

Hollins Farm, Holmfirth Road, Greenfield. The original building ended by the rain water down-pipe, where the quoins can be seen. The barn door has now been raised.

Briarfield Cottage, Sandy Lane, Dobcross. The blocked barn door is to the left of the door. Note the now blocked 'larp-holes' in the wall above the door.

Delph Slack Farm. Built by Robert Whitehead in 1745.

Delph Slack Farm. To the left of the four-light window is the former threashing door. Near the tree are two quoin stones marking the end of the original building.

Delph Slack Farm. Extension to the north side of the original building.

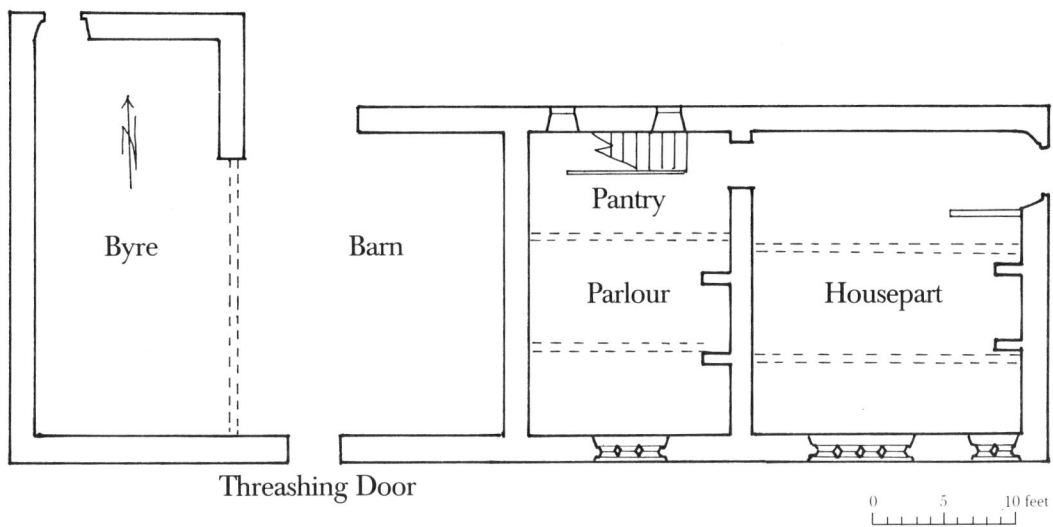

Delph Slack Farm. Plan of ground floor, as built. A further bay was added to the east in the later eighteenth century and the byre extended to the west.

Foulrakes, Greenfield. View from the south-east.

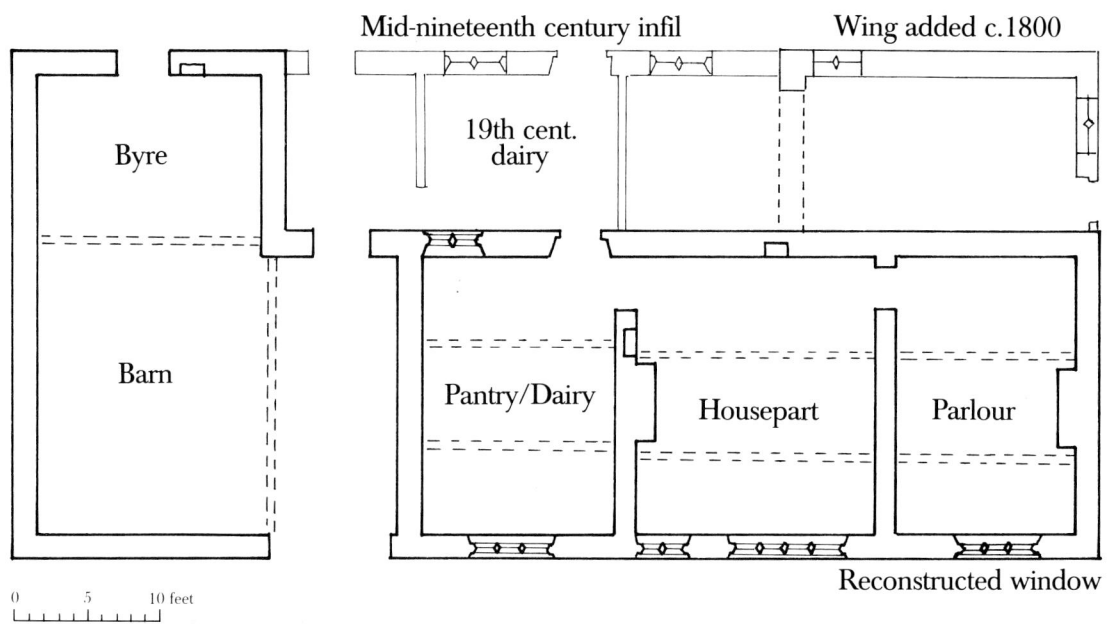

Mid-nineteenth century infil

Wing added c.1800

19th cent. dairy

Byre

Barn

Pantry/Dairy

Housepart

Parlour

Reconstructed window

0   5   10 feet

Foulrakes, Greenfield. Ground floor plan.

above. The threshing door is now a window for a room made out of the east bay of the barn and the north side of the barn has been much altered when the wall was brought out to be in line with the extended bay of the byre. Delph Slack was to have further changes in the early nineteenth century.

A similar arrangement of house and laithe with extended byre is Foulrakes in Greenfield. Over the entrance into the house, carved into the lintel are the initials of John and Mary Andrew and the date 1746. The plan is a departure from the typical Saddleworth house. It is larger being of three bays, and besides having a housepart and parlour, there is an additional bay to the west. Entrance into the house is via a doorway in the north wall leading directly into this west bay, there is no through passage nor lobby entrance. What happened here is a local solution to extending the accommodation in a new building by adhering to the local tradition for a gable entrance and adding a room enclosing that access to the housepart within the third bay. This additional bay was unheated and may have been a pantry or dairy. There is another example of this plan form at Wellihole Cottage, Friezeland, which has the date and initials 1722, J S M S on the door lintel. This entrance too is on the north side and leads direct into what would have been the service room of this three-bay house which is not a laithehouse.[60] Outside the area there is a similar plan at Rodwell End West Farm, Eastwood near Todmorden, dated 1722.

Barns with low wide doorways continued to be built up to the late 1770's. At Hollins Cottage, Greenfield, built c.1740 as a typical two-bay Saddleworth house, a laithe was added to the west in 1776. This had a low wide barn door with a threashing door at the rear (now replaced by a window). The byre was at a lower level than the barn due to the ground falling away to the west (as was the case at Bank Top) and because of the nature of the site it was entered from the west gable end, quite unusual for the area. This laithe is dated 1776 on the roof truss. A reverse case occurs at Stonebreaks where a former laithe (with door now blocked) was added to at a right-angle by the two-bay house recently known as the Parsonage and referred to above. Some twenty and more years later laithes became larger and the barn doors were constructed with semicircular or segmental arches as at Higher Cross Farm where the laithe was added to a two-bay house built in 1746 by the Radcliffe family and at Edge End, Dobcross, where a laithe house was built by Benjamin Lawton shortly after 1791. This house also has a segmental arch to the barn door, which faces north to the fields behind the house.[61] Carts may by then have become more common and made more practicable with better roads and farm tracks. Knott Hill Farm, built in 1771 as a laithehouse, has a segmented arch to the barn. This gives an indication as to when the arched barn door was introduced to Saddleworth.

That grain production was important in the domestic economy is supported by the former existence of corn-drying kilns, usually indicated by field names but supported by a small piece of evidence still surviving in a field boundary near Boarshurst. Here a stile was built from two long stones which have regular sockets cut along two edges in a similar way to principal floor joists having joints cut to house the secondary floor joists. Similar stones are known in east Lancashire and parts of west Yorkshire and at Winewalls, Trawden in east Lancashire is a corn-drying kiln showing how these stones were used. Here the kiln floor of perforated tiles is supported by thin lengths of stone set in the sockets of the supporting stones, such as the one described above. Beneath was the flue chamber carrying the hot fumes from the fire in a passage hearth to dry the grain. This stone construction made the kiln fireproof. A complete corn-drying kiln has not yet been identified in Saddleworth.

A rare example of bee-boles, where beehives were sheltered from the winds, is to be found at Rough Meadow Head, near Delph. Four bee-boles were built into the wall beneath the four-light parlour window to a depth of sixteen inches. They are now blocked up. Honey

Foulrakes, Greenfield. The first extension of a rear wing with, beyond, an early nineteenth-century infilling.

Foulrakes, Greenfield. The datestone over the original entrance into the building. Having been indoors for over one hundred and fifty years, it is in good condition.

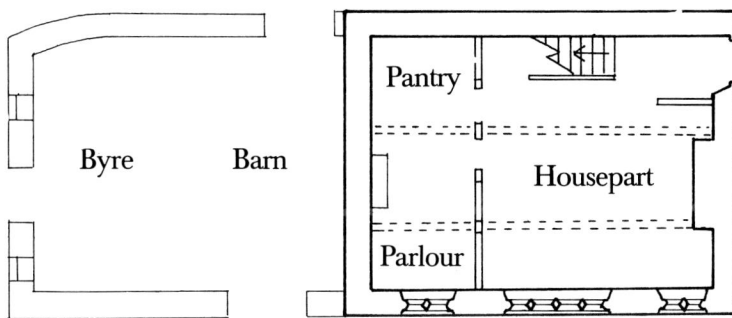

Byre   Barn

Pantry

Housepart

Parlour

0   5   10 feet

Chamber   Chamber

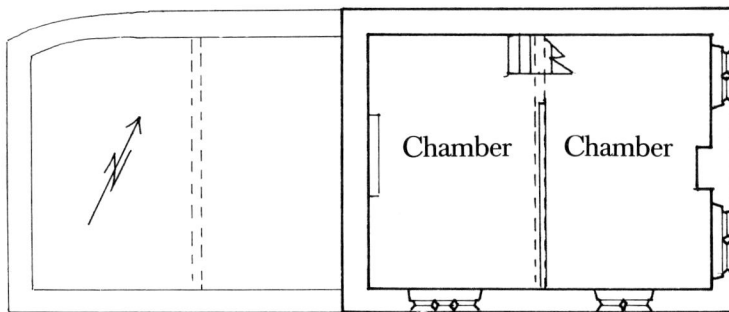

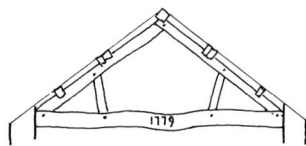

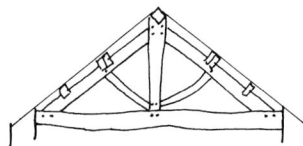

Roof truss in barn   Roof truss in house

1779

Hollins Cottage, Greenfield. Ground floor plan and elevation as existing, circa 1776.

Hollins Cottage, Greenfield. View from the south-east.

Higher Cross Farm. The laithe – barn and byre – added to the house of 1746 at the end of the eighteenth century.

Edge End, Dobcross. Built shortly after 1791. The threashing door is to the right of the parlour window.

Edge End, Dobcross. Rear view showing the segmented arch to the barn door.

Knott Hill Farm, Delph. View from the south. Dating from 1771 it remains very much as built.

Remains of a stone floor-joist from a corn drying kiln. Near Boarshurst. The site has not been identified.

Rough Meadow Head, Delph. Bee-holes built into the wall of the house beneath the parlour window. They are now blocked up, but their outline can still be seen.

would still be a necessary sweetener in the diet of the time and there may have been more bee-holes in Saddleworth. Hives are mentioned in some Saddleworth inventories and these would have been skeps made from coiled straw rather than wooden hives with removable combs. The climate of the west Pennines was suitable for bee keeping for there are few extremes of temperature and bees could survive the winter. In addition to the usefulness of honey as a sweetener the keeping of bees would have been a further instance of a secondary or tertiary source of income.[62]

In 1770 John Lees drew up a survey of the lands owned by James Farrer, the Lord of the Manor. These covered roughly one-third of Quickmere, Shawmere and Lordsmere; Friarmere being ommitted since Farrer did not hold land there. The details given of each property, whether it is new, old, repaired, ruinous, the number of bays of building and outbuilding, are of the utmost importance in the study of Saddleworth buildings, even though it is not a complete coverage of the township.[63]

The buildings are described by the number of bays and occasionally the number of families living in them are recorded, also whether they are new or lately built and if they are old or ancient and perhaps thatched. Seven old houses were thatched as were also eight outhouses (use not specified). It is very probable that these particular buildings were of cruck construction which would normally have a steeper roof pitch than that required for stone flags. Thatch needs to be used on a roof pitch of nearer 50 degrees to help the rain and snow quickly run off and so prevent the water from penetrating through the thatch to the discomforture of the inhabitants beneath.

There were 24 old houses and 5 old cottages, while 75 new houses were mentioned. There were 47 barns of which 9 were new and 6 'ancient', 36 shippons (laithes) which included 6 new and 5 old ones and 4 cowhouses, 3 stables plus an old kiln, all testifying to the agricultural activities of this time. 6 turf cotes, including one new and one fallen down, were used for storing one of the fuels used in the home, dried turfs from the commons. A brewhouse and a cote for ashes, perhaps a privy, are also recorded. There is mention of a woolshop, one old shop and four new shops no doubt relating to the additional occupations, shop meaning a workshop. Except for the first, their use is not specified but it is very probable that they too were workshops for textiles, housing spinning wheels and looms.

This survey presents part of Saddleworth on the eve of the Industrial Revolution, an area already very much involved in a profitable dual economy, hence the amount of new building, but with some links with its past remaining in the ancient thatched buildings. But they were not to survive much longer.

Oakdene Cottage, Deanhead. Note the inserted five-light window on the first floor. The central light is wider than its companions.

Oakdene Cottage, Deanhead. The queen-post truss in the loomshop replacing the former stone party wall.

Chapter 5. The Period Of The Industrial Revolution, c.1770–c.1840

The combination of a series of technological inventions and developing markets overseas led to the late eighteenth century phenomenon of the Industrial Revolution which helped Britain become the first industrial nation in the world, exporting considerable quantities of manufactured goods to all continents.

The contribution made by the north of England was to develop the textile industry by exploiting new inventions in textile machinery which increased the output of cloth, and improvements were made in communications to market towns where there were cloth halls such as at Leeds (1711), Huddersfield (1766), Colne (1773), and Halifax (1779).

The process of improving textile production had begun half a century earlier with John Kay's Fly Shuttle, patented in 1733, which enabled weavers to increase output and made it easier to weave broadcloths. This invention took time to be accepted and its full potential could not be realised until the production of yarn could be equally increased. It was not until 1767 that this was achieved by James Hargreaves' invention of the Spinning Jenny. The jenny was originally intended to spin cotton yarn suitable for wefts in fustian, a cotton-linen fabric then being produced in large quantities by handloom weavers in Lancashire. The jenny as adapted for the woollen trade was found to be an efficient machine for spinning the soft, full woollen yarn required, it was also simple to construct and relatively cheap and so was available to the small manufacturer and clothier working in his own house.[64] The very qualities which made it easily available to clothiers produced great numbers of pirated jennys which denied Hargreaves a just financial return for his important invention, and he died in poverty in 1778.[65]

The jenny could operate up to eighty spindles or more and the possibility of greatly increasing output of cloth by the combination of the spinning-jenny and the fly-shuttle led to an increase in the profits to be made from the textile trade and to considerable changes in the organisation of the industry. The jenny became widespread in Yorkshire after 1770 and caused the ratio of spinners to weavers to fall from ten to one in 1717 to four to one in 1776.

Ammon Wrigley refers to the jenny in his own family's home in his poem entitled 'The Homestead'.

> "There stood upstairs an old hand-loom,
>   Close by my parents' bed,
> A cuckoo clock with flowered face,
>   And heavy weights of lead;
> The fifty-jenny – my mother span,
>   The skips and slubbing creel,
> The "chovin dish," the sizing pan,
>   The twelve-staved bobbin wheel."[66]

The structure of the woollen industry in Saddleworth provides an interesting contrast to the better known system of production adopted in the worsted trade around Halifax. The contrasting systems of organisation produced different architectural responses. The worsted trade requires long stapled wool which was best spun by Arkwright's Water Frame rather than Hargreaves' Spinning-Jenny. The Water Frame was from the first a factory machine relying upon water power, whereas the jenny always remained hand-driven and therefore essentially domestic. So in the worsted trade the spinning went into factories in the late eighteenth century and the worsted weavers' cottages were built in the Halifax area, in such places as Heptonstall, with the loomshop on the top floor with provision for only one or two handlooms, the weavers collecting their warp and weft from the mills.

Site of
Stairs

Site of
Stairs

Inglenook | Housepart

New
fireplace

Housepart

As built c.1742

As altered c.1800

Gable
rebuilt

Site of
smoke
hood

New flue

Gable
rebuilt

First floor converted into a loomshop c.1800

0   5   10 feet

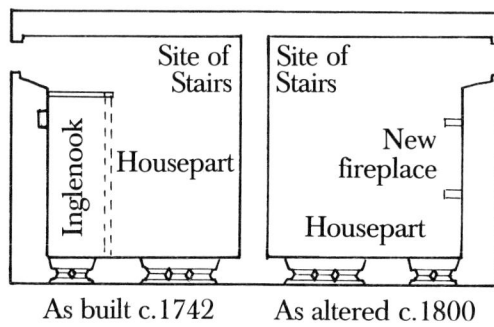

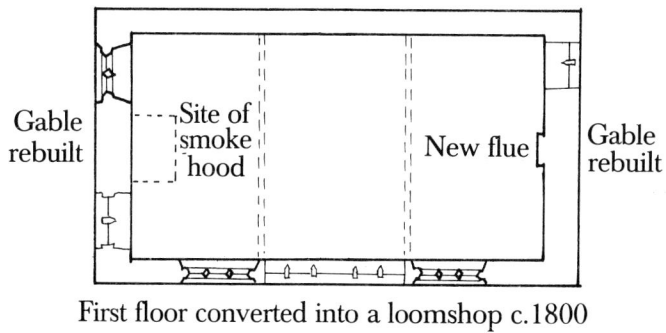

Oakdene Cottage, Deanhead. Plans of ground and first floor following the alterations.

This was the well-known 'putting out' system, the weavers being employees working for the master clothier and often living in long rows of cottages built by the employer. Saddleworth cloth was a superfine broadcloth which, like other woollens, was produced from yarn spun on a jenny. The jenny and the handloom were relatively cheap, could both be accommodated in the home and both required no other power than human muscle. Because of this, many Saddleworth clothiers retained their independence well into the nineteenth century and the industry produced a characteristic weaver's loomhouse with a loomshop spacious enough not only to accommodate looms but also a jenny, warping frame, bobbin winder and other machinery required for the production of woollen cloth.

William Radcliffe, writing of the 1780's, sets the scene dramatically,

". . . while the old loomshops being insufficient, every lumber room, even old barns, cart houses and outbuildings of every description were repaired, windows broke through the old blank walls, and all fitted up for loomshops. This source of making room being at length exhausted, new weaver's cottages with loomshops rose up in every direction, all immediately filled."[67]

Radcliffe was writing about the cotton industry in Mellor in north east Cheshire, but his observations refer just as well to the area between the Lancashire plain and the Vale of York.

The changes made to the buildings of Saddleworth as a result of the introduction of machines in cloth making, are to be seen everywhere. Hardly a pre-1790 building is untouched, all show evidence of alterations designed to increase the working accommodation and facilities.

The Loomshop

A good example to start with is Oakdene Cottage at Deanhead, already described as a rare example of a dual house, built circa 1742. The changes here involved opening out the upper floors of both cottages to extend the loomshop to the full length of the building. This meant that each cottage lost its private upper chamber, privacy giving way to profit. The party wall was taken down to ground floor ceiling level and replaced by a new roof truss. Between the original three-light windows on the upper floors of each cottage was added a five-light window with the central light wider than the two on either side. This was to accommodate a vertical sash window for reasons which will be explained later.

Owing to the sharp rise of the land to the rear there are no windows on that side. At first floor level in both gable ends there are two two-light windows, one being added at the period of rebuilding. These 'cross-light' windows would have helped to give light to the otherwise dark corners of the loomshop. From the front elevation it is clear how much the building was heightened. The new coursing is easily recognised, five courses which are wider and more regular than the earlier walling.

What is not so evident is how much the two gable ends were altered. Careful observation shows that they were taken down to within five to six feet of the ground. But this would not be necessary if it was only to incorporate two new windows at first floor level. A clue is inside the southern gable end, a small cupboard in the wall about four feet from the floor. The ground floor rooms each have a two-light fireside window associated with an inglenook against the gable wall, a feature also associated with a wall cupboard. In this event there would have been a timber wattle and daub smoke hood over the inglenook

Lower Delph Slack, Delph. View from the north-west. The lower window on the left has a flag-stone inner lintel.

Lower Delph Slack, Delph. Detail of window. Note the different texture of the flagstone to the gritstone jambs.

which, in the room above, would have taken up floor space. So to remove this and completely open out the first floor rooms, the smoke hoods were removed, the gable walls taken down far enough to enable a narrow, stone flue to be incorporated within the new wall together with a new fireplace. The flue projects some three to four inches from the inside of the gable wall. This work would have been done circa 1800.

A similar change occurred at Lower Grange at the same time and also at Bank Top where a new fireplace and flue replaced the former inglenook, the oven which had projected from the gable end, was removed, suggesting that the technique of baking bread was changing, perhaps using a bakestone or griddle.[68]

The practice of removing former partition walls at first floor level demanded the insertion of new roof trusses. These were normally of the queen post truss type with the purlins butted to the principal rafter, with a tongue passing through the rafter and pegged on the further side. This becomes a widespread technique of joining purlins to roof trusses from the turn of the century. At Golcar, just to the north of Saddleworth, there are several in a range of buildings dated 1842 and 1844.[69]

With the upper floor opened out to be used as a loomshop, no doubt by all the occupiers of the former cottages, additional windows were required. In addition to the extra two-light windows added to each gable at first floor level, a five-light window was built between the original three-light windows on this upper floor. These new windows featured changes in the regional building traditions. The mullions now presented a square section to the outer face and are roughly chamfered inside. The simple section was much easier to cut than the previously used cavetto section. The reason for this change is clearly the dictates of mass production. The change occurs in the Pennines in the 1780's and is in full swing by the turn of the century. An examination of the buildings throughout Saddleworth and the adjoining areas show clearly the vast amount of building and rebuilding done between the 1780's and the mid-nineteenth century. The amount of material required would call for some streamlining in the supply of stone for walls, windows and doorways, so standard size walling stone appears together with the plain, square section mullions.

To speed up the process of manufacturing mullions, the use of the Coal Measures stone flags was sometimes resorted to, the stone splitting easily to the required thickness and depth. The disadvantage of this material has only become apparent a century or so later when, through the action of the weather and pressure of the weight above, these mullions have split or spalled and decayed along their lower end.

In Saddleworth, the tradition of recessing the mullions from the face of the wall continues in conjunction with the use of inner lintels which are often separate from the main lintel above. The earliest example of the use of flagstone in a window is at Lower Delph Slack, dated 1760, where flagstone is used for the inner lintel, the remainder of the window being made of gritstone. The use of flagstone did not become universal in Saddleworth, being mainly found in the valleys and on the lower slopes.

Returning to Oakdene Cottage, the new five-light window incorporated a new feature for the time, a small, vertical sash window. This central light is slightly wider than its companions to either side, so allowing room for the wooden sash frame. Only the lower part of the window was moveable and, not being counter-balanced, when raised was held up by a piece of wood. The purpose of this window was to help ventilate the loomshop and similar examples are to be found throughout the woollen cloth manufacturing area in the Pennines from the Ribble Valley down to north Derbyshire.

Temperature and humidity levels are not critical for the working of wool in contrast to cotton, but it is important to maintain an even temperature and humidity level throughout the time it takes to weave a piece of cloth, otherwise the tension would change and the weave become tighter or slacker through the length of cloth and so have a serious effect

New Tame, Delph. Early and late traditions of mullion windows.

Pinfold. One of the taking-in doors on the west front. There may have been a simple hoist attached to the lintel.

Pinfold. The west front showing the changes of stonework as a result of increasing the loomshop accommodation.

on its quality. A window and a small fireplace were the means by which the atmosphere of the woollen loomshop could be maintained. If there was no provision for a fireplace then a small brazier was used, such as the one formerly at Deanhead.

A dramatic instance of the change of window design in a loomshop is to be seen at New Tame where the seven-light cavetto section mullion window, complete with a hood mould, remains from the late seventeenth century house which was rebuilt and heightened incorporating the newer square section mullions with wider lights at first floor level. The roughly trimmed splays to the new style mullions were covered by plaster as part of the finish to the interior which was then whitewashed to reflect the light inside.

Oakdene Cottage was adapted to the woollen industry in one extensive rebuilding operation, but many houses suffered much more piecemeal adaptation. At Pinfold the remains of the late seventeenth century house can be identified at ground floor level in the design of the windows with hood mould and the use of large stones in the walling.[70]

In the early eighteenth century the west wall of the parlour was rebuilt incorporating an elegant window which still largely remains. The first major changes were at the first floor level over the housepart where a new loomshop was made by raising the walls and putting in a new range of windows, one with six lights on the west wall, a four-light window on the east wall and two two-light windows in the gable. Shortly after this, the upper west wall of the parlour bay was rebuilt from the first floor to include a 'taking-in' door.

Taking-in doors were a new feature to Saddleworth and other areas where the domestic industry was practiced. Where domestic life and industry have to co-exist, it is clearly an advantage to have separate means of access to each working part of the house. As woollen cloth was made on the upper floors it was common sense to provide a direct access to the loomshop via an outer door to this upper floor, this doorway could have been provided with a simple hoist for lifting the bales of wool and lowering the woven cloth. The remains of hoists can be seen at the rear of the house at the corner of Stonewood Road and Grains Road, and in the gable of number 10 King Street, both in Delph. Steps could be provided for the weavers and cloth workers and some impressive examples are to be seen at Higher Kinders and Lower Tunstead Farm. Where the ground rose steeply behind the building, a bridge, using a large stone flag or of timber construction, would give access from the higher ground direct to the upper loomshop. Few of these remain but it is clear that they were used at the rear of High Kinders, Ballgreave and Nettlehole among others.

Following the building of a new loomshop and taking-in door at Pinfold, a complete new upper storey was built at the end of the eighteenth or beginning of the nineteenth century. This had a window of thirteen lights on the west, a pair of two-light windows in both gable ends and a three-light plus a four-light window on the east. Internal access to this large loomshop was by a staircase that came up in the centre of the floor area, an important consideration when it is realised just how precious was the need to use all the light from the windows for the benefit of the weavers at their looms. A staircase coming up by an external wall would use some of this valuable floor space by a window which could have been occupied by a loom. The normal practice was therefore to have the stairs coming up in the middle of the room, away from any wall.

The final phase of building at Pinfold occurred in the early nineteenth century when a complete house and loomshop was added to the north, so blocking the north gable windows of the earlier loomshop. This new building was entirely self-contained and there was no internal connection with the earlier building. The taking-in door at first floor level on the west front is now blocked, but once led direct to the staircase leading from this floor to the loomshop above and alongside the former gable wall which had become a party wall.

All the roof trusses are queen post trusses supporting two purlins on each side, but

Top row, left to right:

Houseparte — Built c.1800

Parlour — Built c.1720

Housepart — Built c.1660

Middle row, left to right:

Chamber

Taking-in Door

Chamber

Taking-in Door

Chamber

Bottom row, left to right:

Loomshop

Loomshop

0   5   10 feet

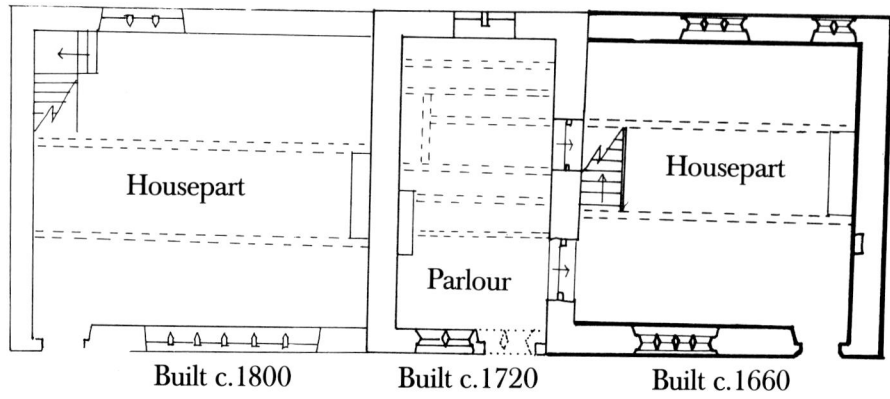

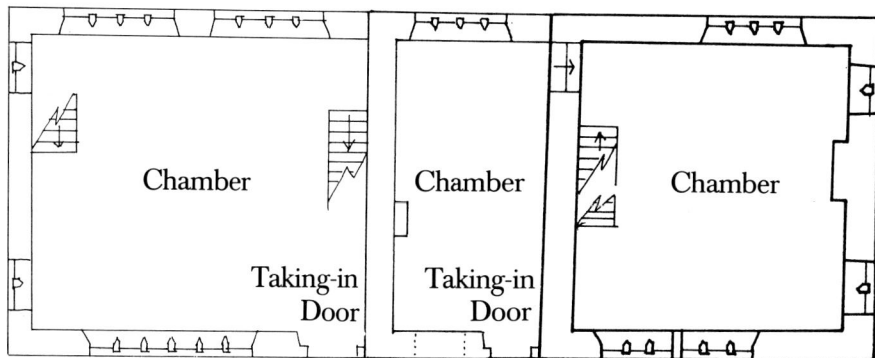

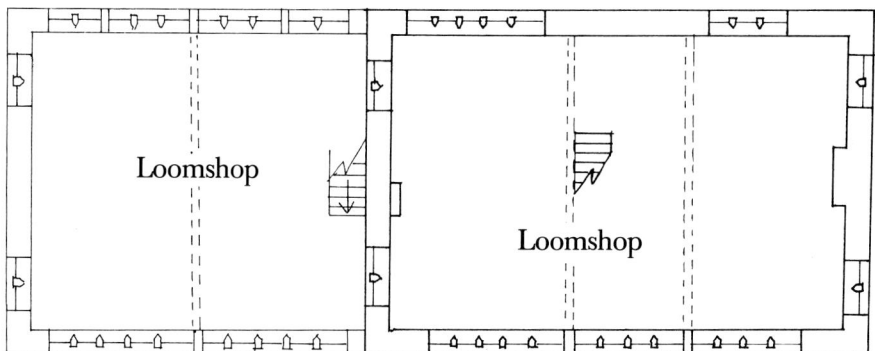

Pinfold. Plan of the three floors.

Barn at Pinfold. View from the north-west.

The Cottage, Running Hill. The reverse of the
two coins found during alterations in 1977.

here they follow an earlier form of construction in being half-lapped over the top edge of the principal rafters. New ideas in building were not necessarily accepted all at once.

Such was the demand for working space that the barn at Pinfold also underwent some reconstruction. In the north bay a fireplace was built onto the north gable and a further loomshop made on the upper floor, formerly a loft over the byres. This loomshop was given an unusual set of windows, two four-light windows one immediately above the other.

Rebuilding upper floors to increase working accommodation was widely practised and it is also well illustrated at Butterhouse, built in 1719. Here the ground floor and first floor remain more or less intact and, as at Pinfold, a complete new loomshop has been added as a third floor. A further example is the Cottage at Running Hill, built in the early eighteenth century. Here the whole of the upper floor was rebuilt and provision made for a loft in the roof space illuminated by a two-light window in the west gable. These lofts were used for storing materials and spare parts. They usually extended eight to ten feet from a gable end with the inner end supported by iron stirrups from the purlins if it did not extend to a convenient wall or roof truss.

When alterations were being made at the Cottage in 1977, a first floor window was removed and under the sill were found two coins, both pennies, one Irish, dated 1769 and the other an English one dated 1774. Both were very worn. This suggests that the upper floor was raised after 1780 – accounting for the state of the coins – and when the sill was being set in place these coins were carefully laid on the joint as a momento or as a token to ensure good fortune to the household.

> "Three horse shoes on the shippon door –
> To keep the hag away,
> That "witched" the cows and spoiled the milk
> In my grandfather's day." [71]

Evidence of lofts is often to be seen in the small rectangular openings about one foot wide and one and a half feet high, set near the apex of the gable, often on both sides of a chimney flue. These can be seen at Holden Smithy on Spurn Lane, Diggle, in the north gable. The raising of the upper floor here is clearly shown in the wider coursing used and by the introduction of a taking-in door on the lane side. These changes were preceded by the building of a pair of independent loomshops to the south. The process of development is clearly seen from the east, the vertical break at ground floor level showing where the quoins have been removed and the new building butted up to the older one with some attempt at bonding eight feet above ground level. The quoins at the north east and west corners indicate the original height of the walls to the earlier house, but returning to the east front it can be seen that quoins are used on the top north east corner of the new pair of loomshops, not butted up to by the heightened first floor of the original building. So the new loomshops were built before the upper floor of the earlier building was reconstructed to carry a twelve-light window to the east, a pair of two-light windows in the north gable and three windows of four, three and two lights respectively on the west wall. The section of walling above these windows six courses up to the eaves, is a further indication that there was provision for a loft in this part of the building.

William Radcliffe made reference to the conversion of old barns and outbuildings into loomshops and an example of this survived at what is now known as Ash Cottage, Boarshurst. This had formerly been a byre and signs of its former function can be seen in the blocked ventilating holes in the south gable and east wall. As a byre it was small, with the walls rising only ten feet to the eaves. The outline of the original gables is still to be clearly seen by the change in the depth of the coursing of the later additions to heighten the building. On the east side, the original entrance survives, but now blocked. This has a triangular-headed lintel supported on built up jambs, the right-hand one of which projects into the door space to the height of two courses. The reason for this is not clear. A later

Holden Smithy, Spurn Lane, Diggle. View from the south-east.

Holden Smithy, Spurn Lane, Diggle. View from the north. The heightening of the loomshop is very clear. Note the blocked windows for the loft.

Ash Cottage, Boarshurst, Greenfield. The original door to the byre is near the corner. The blocked larp-holes can be made out in the earlier masonry.

Ash Cottage, Boarshurst, Greenfield. View from the south.

New Tame, Delph. Number 5 is on the right.

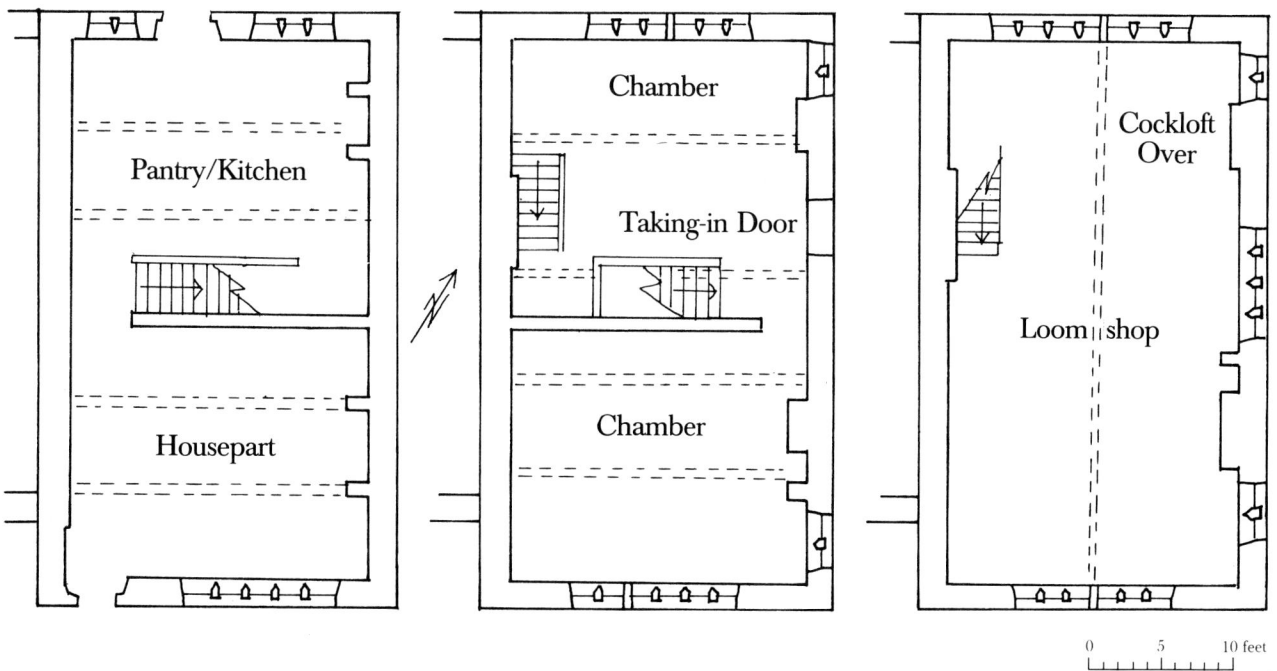

Number 5 New Tame, Delph. Plans of the three floors. In recent years the loomshop has been subdivided.

doorway lies to the right of this and gives access to the cottage. This conversion gave a housepart and parlour on the ground floor with the former lit by a five-light window and the latter by a three-light window while the first floor was open from end to end with an eight-light window in the west wall, a two-light window in the east wall and a two-light window in the north gable. All the windows have the square section mullions which are recessed from the plane of the wall in the typical Saddleworth tradition. These mullions are heavy in character and would suggest a date of circa 1800.

The Developed Loomshop

By the turn of the century the purpose-built loomshop was well established in Saddleworth. At New Tame the process of adaption and change often incorporating old materials culminated at the north end of the row (number 5) with a large three-storey one-bay house, two rooms deep. But even this imposing building, ostensibly of one build, made use of an earlier structure the remains of which can be seen at ground floor level in the north gable wall. This could have been a byre.

Entrance is directly from the front into the house, the parlour cum kitchen is at the rear with the staircase between the two rooms. This leads only to the first floor. On this floor is the taking-in door, now blocked, in the north gable. To reach the loomshop there is a staircase against the party wall giving access within the loomshop, well away from the working areas by the windows. The loomshop is well lit by a six-light window on the east and a seven-light window on the west, each window having a king mullion extending the full depth of the wall, which supports the roof truss. On the north gable end, in addition to two cross-light windows, there is a four-light window with a two-light window above; this latter window was for the loft which had been partially supported by iron stirrups. One light in each window had a sash opening, all the others were fixed, and at the southern end of the loomshop is a small fireplace insufficient for heating this large open room but adequate for maintaining even working temperatures.

The roof truss is very impressive, spanning thirty-two feet between the walls. It is a queen post truss but because of its length there are subsidiary posts, sometimes known as 'Princess posts', between the tiebeam and principal rafter, all carrying diagonal braces. Because of the size of the truss with its long pitch from the ridge to the eaves, there are four purlins per pitch which are butt jointed to the principal rafter and held by a tonge passing through the rafter pegged on the far side. A roof truss of similar size and design is to be found at Dale Head House, built in the 1820's, but here the room was probably used as a warehouse with access by a staircase from first floor level at the rear.

The size of the timbers necessary for this truss, and others in Saddleworth, raises the question of the availability of such large trees necessary to provide them. In 1795 John Aikin observed,

> "The houses are all built of stone, which is in great plenty; but timber comes high, being brought from Hull or Liverpool, and undergoing an expensive land carriage." [72]

He then goes on to point out that the new Huddersfield Canal passing through Saddleworth would ease the problem of transport. By August 1797 this canal had reached Uppermill where for some years it ended at Woolroad wharf, until the tunnel through to Marsden was completed in 1811.

Timber was being imported at this time from both North America and the Baltic countries through Hull and Liverpool and some of the smaller ports on the coasts such as Skipool on the river Wyre. At Liverpool the southern end of the docks had become known as "Timber Town" in the late eighteenth century. Here the timber was sawn into various sizes and lengths before being transported to its final destination by road, river or canal.[73]

Number 5 New Tame, Delph. Interior of loomshop. The small fireplace is in the chimney flue.

Number 5 New Tame, Delph. The small fireplace in the loomshop.

Number 5 New Tame, Delph. The queen-post truss with princess-posts, all braced. Note the bolt heads under the tie-beam and iron strap on the queen-post.

Cherry Clough House, Denshaw. Example of the incised cyphers which are widespread throughout Saddleworth in buildings dating from circa 1800.

During the Napoleonic Wars, timber came principally from Canada and was imported duty free until 1821. As a result, imports from the Baltic states dropped, from 99% in 1788 to 24% in 1833, of the total imports of timber through Liverpool. There are signs that a substantial amount of imported timber used in Saddleworth in the early nineteenth century came from the Baltic countries. This was mainly softwood such as pine and was used mainly for roof trusses and floor joists, and sometimes for purlins. It is to be noted that some sense of thrift was practiced in Saddleworth where use of wood was concerned. While buildings were becoming wider the distance between trusses remained the same as before and so old oak purlins could be and were re-used.

On many exposed floor joists and tiebeams there are to be seen scratched or incised cyphers which bear no relationship to the normal form of letters or numerals. There is a very fine display of these on some of the upper floor joists of number 2 High Kinders; they also occur on joists at Fur Lane Farm Cottage, Cherry Clough House, on both tiebeams there, and on tiebeams in barns at Red Lane Farm and Platt Hill, Dobcross, to indicate a few. The cyphers appear to relate to a form of cyrillic (or glagolithic) alphabet used by Baltic countries including Russia, and they could be consignment markings from the port of origin.

The Double-Pile Loomhouse

In the early nineteenth century a larger type of loomhouse makes an appearance. This has a double-pile plan where in addition to the usual house plus parlour plan arrangement, there is another range of rooms at the rear, so giving a plan two rooms deep. This increased the accommodation providing for the possibility of a separate kitchen and pantry, or dairy, or a change in the position of the fireplace. It also gave a much larger loomshop on the top floor.

Deanhead at the top of Harrop Dale is a unique survival of a clothier's establishment in Saddleworth. Here is his loomhouse with a dyehouse and cropping shed all surviving, plus some evidence of fulling stocks. From Oakdene Cottage the Rhodes family moved to this new large purpose-built loomhouse at Deanhead at the turn of the nineteenth century, a clear indication of the success of this family enterprise. The tradition of mullion windows is maintained; the taking-in door is at first floor level in the west gable near to the rising ground and the loomshop is well lit by a series of windows in all the walls. A blocked two-light window in each gable suggests a former loft. The staircase rises alongside the central wall through the first two floors and so enters the loomshop in the centre of the vast open space.

This loomshop was photographed about 1910 before the contents were sold to Halifax Corporation for the Bankfield Museum (they are now to be seen in the Piece Hall Museum). This photograph published in 1912 shows a multi-spindle jenny, a bobbin winder (formerly a great spinning wheel), warping frames and two hand-looms which have been braced to the tiebeams of the roof trusses by splints.[74] In the foreground is a charcoal brazier which was the means of controlling the working temperature and humidity. The windows show their original glazing of small, rectangular panes of glass approximately five inches by eight inches, arranged three panes wide and six deep, the glass being held in lead cames which in turn are held in the window opening by means of horizontal glazing bars which were usually iron, although wood was also used.

By the entrance into the loomhouse is a small single-storey wing which was the dairy. Below the house to the east is another single-storey building of two bays which was the dyehouse; there were stone troughs inside but these are now covered over. In the fields behind are many springs supplying clear, soft water. In the valley below are the remains of the fulling stocks once driven by a water wheel taking its power from the small mill

Deanhead, Harrop Dale. View from the south. The wing on the left is a former warehouse. Behind is a barn and byre.

Deanhead, Harrop Dale. The interior of the loomshop photographed circa 1910 when the contents were acquired by Halifax Corporation.

Deanhead, Harrop Dale. Oakdene Cottage is beyond Deanhead. In the foreground is the former dyehouse.

Marled Earth Farm, near New Tame. View from the south. The walls and mullions have been rendered.

Marled Earth Farm, near New Tame. Rear view. Notice the wider lights in the eleven-light window. The central light would have had a sash window.

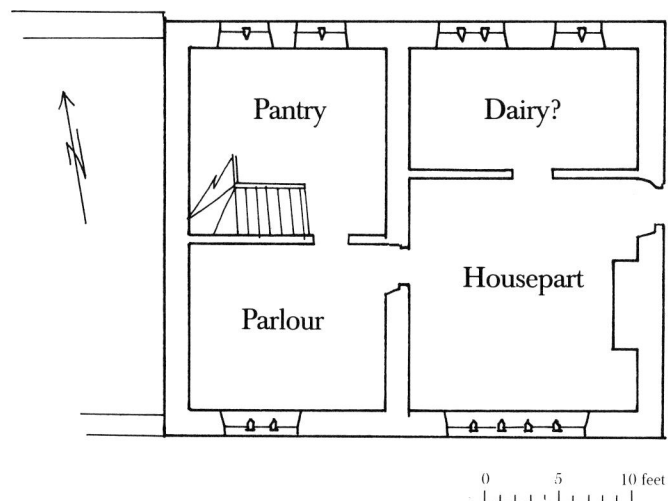

Marled Earth Farm, near New Tame. Plan of ground floor.

Red Lane Farm, Carr Lane, Diggle. A double-pile loomhouse with gable entrance.

Red Lane Farm, Carr Lane, Diggle. Part of a queen-post roof truss. Note the smaller scantling of the timbers.

Pantry/Dairy   Larder?

Housepart   Parlour

Loomshop

Taking-in Door

0   5   10 feet

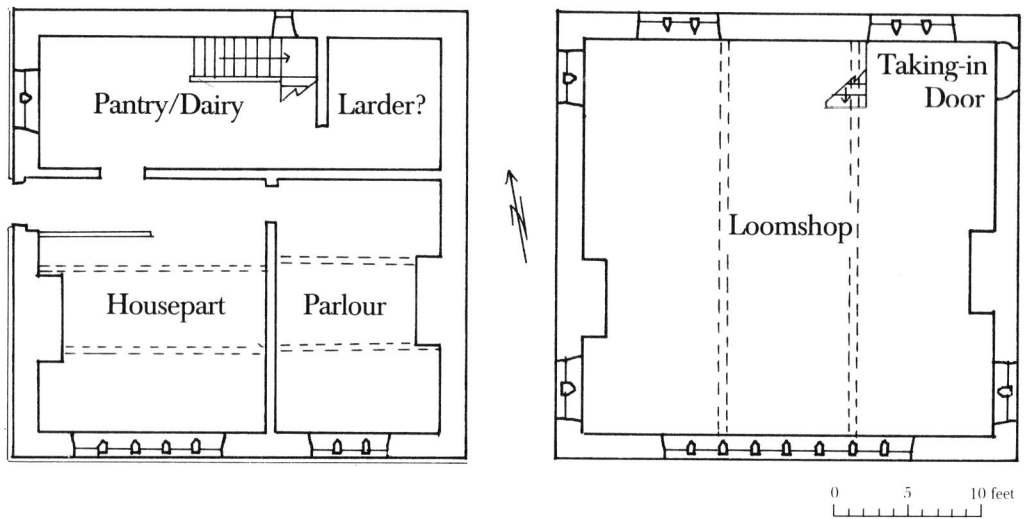

Red Lane Farm, Carr Lane, Diggle. Plan of ground and upper floor.

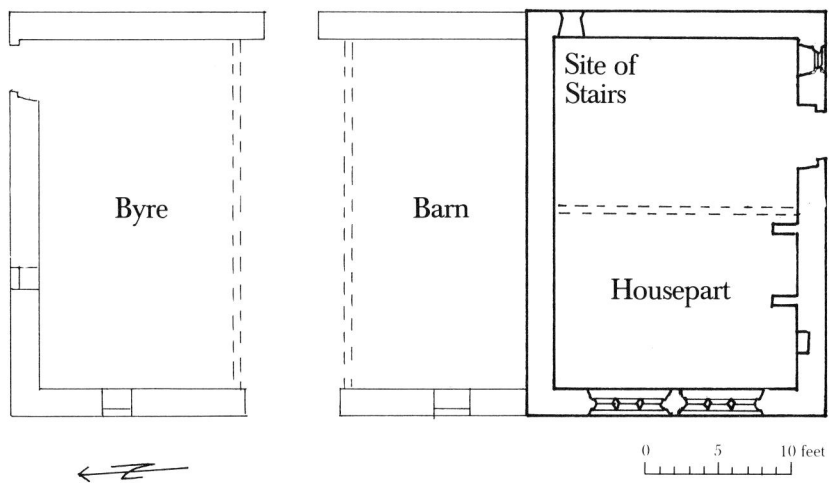

Byre   Barn

Site of Stairs

Housepart

0   5   10 feet

Rye Top, Knowl Top Lane, Uppermill. Plan of ground floor.

dam behind. The dam is now breached and only the wheel pit is readily identified. On the east side of this valley above the fulling stocks were the tenter fields, where the fulled cloth was dried and stretched. Close by is the cropping shed built after 1822,[75] a long narrow single-storey building with five windows on each side to give light on to the cropping benches. Here the woollen cloth was first 'teased' by raising the nap of the cloth using teasles, then it was stretched tightly over the bench and the raised nap removed by cropping shears to produce a smooth surface. The cloth was then ready for marketing. Returning to the loomhouse, a warehouse was added later in the nineteenth century to the west gable end, extending only one bay and half the depth of the loomhouse. The few windows here are similar to those on the nearby cropping shed.

Another double-pile plan loomhouse which still retains some earlier building traditions is Marled Earth near New Tame. The gable entrance gives access to the house alongside the fireplace, to the right is an unheated room with two windows, one of two-lights and the other of three-lights. This room faces north and may have been used as a dairy. Beyond the house is the parlour, also unheated and to the right (north) of this is the pantry and staircase. The pantry has two two-light windows in the manner of the late seventeenth century buildings discussed previously.

The loomshop once occupied the whole of the top floor but has long since been divided into separate rooms. A twelve-light window gives light from the south. These are the traditional narrow lights, one foot six inches wide, but on the north where there is an eleven-light window the lights are wider, one foot nine inches, with the central light being square, no doubt for a sash window. But why this difference in size? The loomhouse appears to be of one build (the south front is rendered and a barn or byre was added to the west) and there are no clear signs of alterations to the fabric. Perhaps the builder had worked out that larger lights on the north side would be more useful for the weaker north light.

A double-pile building without such problems of interpretation is Red Lane Farm off Carr Lane, Diggle, a solid well-built loomhouse built at the beginning of the nineteenth century. A near central gable entrance leads into the house with the parlour beyond, both rooms being heated. From the house there is access to a long narrow room to the north which is unequally divided into two. The first room has a two-light window in the gable wall. At the other end of the room is the staircase rising along the north wall, turning to give access into the loomshop. A small window in the north wall gives some light to the pantry under the stairs. Beyond this room, which may have been a kitchen or dairy, is a small square windowless room. This may have been a store room or larder.

The loomshop occupies the whole of the upper floor. It is very well-lit with a south window of eight lights, two windows of two-lights each on the north wall, two two-light windows in the west gable and one two-light window in the east wall; a taking-in door is in the same gable and leads directly into the loomshop. In each gable are two one-light loft lights but there are no longer any traces of the lofts.

The roof is spanned by two queen post trusses with three purlins per pitch. The trusses and purlins are relatively light in scantling when compared with examples already described and all the timber has been cut by machine which suggests an early nineteenth century date for the construction of this building.

The Single Unit Plan

At the other end of the scale are the one-room loomhouses of which there are many examples in Saddleworth. An early example is at Rye Top off Knowl Top Lane, Uppermill, built at the beginning of the eighteenth century. This is the lower of the two buildings and by the addition of a large barn it has become a laithe house. As usual it has a gable entrance, here in the south gable. To the right of the doorway is a one-light window with moulded

Rye Top, Knowl Top Lane, Uppermill. View from the south. The gable entrance is now blocked, to the right is a one-light window.

Rye Top, Knowl Lane, Uppermill. View from the west showing the large barn added in the early nineteenth century.

Number 15 Harrop Green. View from the south. The upper two-light window is a later feature and so is the square window on the ground floor between the two-light fireside window and the housepart window. The door is also a later feature.

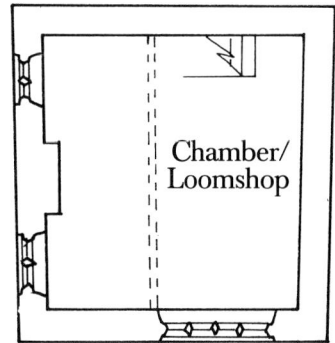

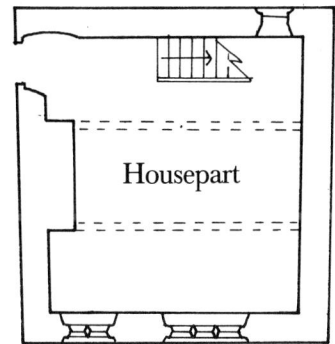

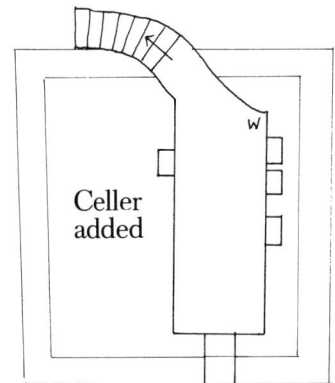

Number 15 Harrop Green. Plan of ground floor and upper floor as built, and the cellar added circa 1800.

Boarshurst Lane, Greenfield. A single-bay cottage very similar to number 15 Harrop Green. Here the gable has been rebuilt but the right-hand jamb to the original entrance still remains at the far right.

Numbers 9 and 11 Sugar Lane, Dobcross. View from the east. The different size coursing indicates the different building periods. Note the heightened gable to number 7 on the extreme right.

jambs and a recessed lintel. The door leads into the house which measures twenty feet by sixteen feet and is lit by a six-light window which has a king mullion on the west wall. The cavetto section mullions are recessed as usual. Internally, on the south gable, is the fireplace and a small wall cupboard to its right. There is no indication that there has ever been an inglenook nor are there any indications of any internal partitioning. A small window in the north-west corner indicates where the former staircase was placed, otherwise there are no windows in the east wall and no signs of any in the former north gable wall. The single window near the door may have been to bring some light into what would have otherwise been a dark corner.

The upper room is unheated and has a four-light window on the west and two two-light windows in the south gable. It is a very simple building affording the means of a basic life-style, but it is not ungenerous in size or mean in its construction.

In the early nineteenth century, and before 1822, the barn was added to the north and an internal doorway cut through the north gable to link both buildings.

The larger building of Rye Top standing to the east was built in the 1820's on the site of an earlier building whose remains can be seen at the rear.

Number 15 Harrop Green is now part of a row of stone cottages and houses, but when built it stood alone. It has a single unit plan eighteen feet square, with a west gable entrance, stairs exist opposite this entrance with a small pantry underneath lit by a small single-light window. The main windows face south; on the ground floor is a two-light fireside window plus a four-light window, all with cavetto section mullions. Owing to the small area of this room it is unlikely that there ever was an inglenook, so the fireside light is there as a purely traditional feature. On the top floor is a four-light window to the south plus two two-light windows in the west gable. If there were windows in the east gable, there are no signs of them now. A queen post truss spans the loomshop. This and the wider lights in the windows, measuring one foot eight inches in width, plus the other features relating to the windows put this building into the 1770's period, perhaps built shortly after the Survey of Saddleworth of 1770.

Later in the history of this house a cellar was built within the outer walls, the entrance being from outside to the north. This cellar has a barrel vaulted ceiling and there are storage niches in the side walls. A deep well in the north-east corner helped to keep the temperature down there cool, for this building became an inn or beerhouse around 1800 known as the Holly Bush, catering for the navvies then building the nearby canal tunnel.

Similar examples of the single unit or bay plan are to be seen at number 25 Huddersfield Road, Diggle; at the house on the junction of Wall Hill Road and Delph New Road at Tame Water; and Brook Cottage also at Tame Water. Some of these small cottages have since been added to, but careful observation will reveal straight joints in the masonry or quoin stones in the middle of a wall identifying the original extent of the building.

This is the case with the group of cottages and loomhouses on Boarshurst Lane. The original single-bay cottage stands at the south-west corner of the group and can be easily identified from the quoins left in situ when the building was extended to the north. It is very similar to number 15 Harrop Green even to the size of the lights in the windows, but here the gable was rebuilt when the cottage was enlarged by a bay which included a new gable entrance on to Boarshurst Lane. The old south gable was rebuilt to include a smaller fireplace with a flue in what became the parlour, replacing the former inglenook. The right-hand jamb of the original door is still visible.

In Dobcross, on Sugar Lane, is a group of single-bay cottages that began with number 7, a two-storey cottage with an entrance in the east gable and a four or five-light window to the south – now blocked. A building on this site appears on the 1770 map, but here it lies at an angle to the road (Sugar Lane) whereas the present complex of cottages are

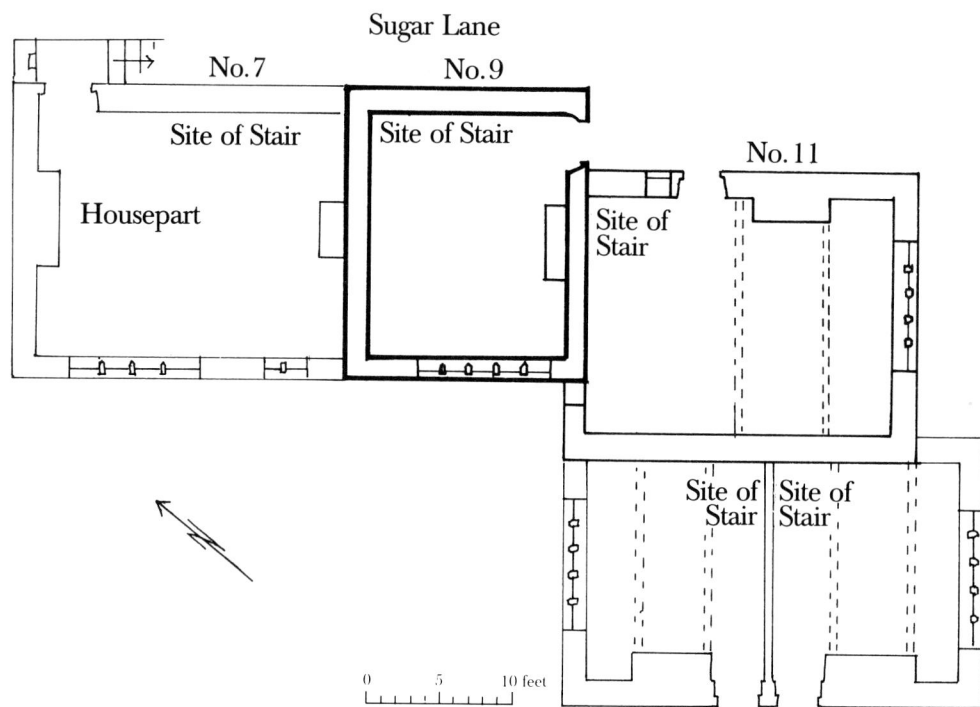

Numbers 7, 9 and 11 Sugar Lane, Dobcross. Plan of ground floor.

Number 11 Sugar Lane, Dobcross. South gable showing the two adjoining doors, now blocked, to the two former cottages.

Hey Top. Greenfield. Known locally as 'Forty Row' after the number of back-to-back cottages built by 1849. Four more were added later but the name stuck.

Hey Top, Greenfield. The four single-bay loomhouses built before 1822. Note how they were heightened when cottages were added to their rear and the whole extended as a row of back-to-back cottages.

parallel to the road. They would therefore post date the 1770 map. Number 7 has been raised a storey and partially refronted. Number 9 was added to the east gable of number 7 but set back to avoid blocking the gable entrance. It then extends to the rear to make up the depth required. The entrance is in the gable which fronts on to the road and is now hidden by a lean-to. Alongside this entrance is a small window which would have been for a small pantry beneath the staircase to the upper floor. In the east wall is a five-light window and in the short length of west wall a small single-light window. The upper floor is lit by two two-light windows in the gable and a three-light window in the east wall.

Behind number 9 was added number 11. This was a 'dual house', two single-bay cottages alongside each other and with adjoining doorways in the south gable. The internal stairs were opposite each door. All this activity was completed by 1822 at the latest. Sometime in the mid-nineteenth century the two cottages were converted into one, the original doors blocked and a new one opened in the projecting north section of the wall.

Between 1800 and 1822 four small single-bay two-storey loomhouses were built at Hey Top above Greenfield Mill which was built in 1794 as a scribbling and fulling mill by John Whitehead, and with which the cottages were no doubt associated. By 1849 they had become part of a row of forty back-to-back cottages for mill workers.[76]

Moston Cottage on Stockport Road, Lydgate, was built soon after 1822. This may well be the last of the single-bay cottages to be built in Saddleworth. It also breaks with tradition in having the entrance on the main (east) front and not in the gable. The house was lit by a six-light window with square section mullions, the centre one being a king mullion. A two-light window to the west of the fireplace would help to give light to an otherwise dark corner (compare with Rye Top). In the corner opposite to the entrance is the staircase turning at right angles halfway in its ascent and giving access to the loomshop midway along the rear wall. There were no internal partitions when built, each floor being an open space, eighteen by fifteen feet. Living and cooking was done in the one ground floor room and sleeping and weaving in the upper room.

It is unlikely that any activity other than weaving was done in these single-bay cottages, two looms would fill the space easily. It can therefore be surmised that such loomhouses were associated with piece-work and it is worth noting that most of the single-bay cottages are in the west part of Saddleworth and near to Oldham where fustian was woven on the piecework system.

Thus by the early nineteenth century there were loomhouses to suit all pockets, from large double-pile three-storey loomhouses to two-storey single-bay loomhouses, but all were built to the same high standards of craftsmanship. In this can be seen a further indication of the independent mind of Saddleworthians of those days, an element of pride in the quality of life they could attain.

The Architecture of Affluence

By the end of the eighteenth century, there appeared signs of change to the long established traditions of building and design. The strongest influence was probably that of classical architecture which came with the building of three chapels of ease within the Chapelry of Saddleworth, at Heights in 1765 and at Dobcross and Lydgate, both in 1788. All three buildings featured Venetian windows in the chancels.

St. Thomas's, Heights, is a typical auditory church of the eighteenth century. Essentially it is a rectangular nave with south, west and north galleries maximising the number who could follow the service conducted from a central two or three-decker pulpit. The chancel is a shallow projection from the east gable containing the altar, lit by a large Venetian window. This has a centre light with semi-circular arch in which there is a bold keystone and on either side narrower lights rising only as far as the spring of the arch of the central

St. Thomas's Chapel, Heights. View from the south-west.

St. Thomas's Chapel, Heights. One of the two west doors dated 1765.

St. Thomas's Chapel, Heights. The chancel window.

Holy Trinity, Dobcross. Built in 1788, the Italianate tower was added in 1843.

Holy Trinity, Dobcross. Decorative tooling on the north-west quoin stones.

Woods House, Dobcross, built in 1782 by John Harrop. The tripartite windows were a new feature introduced into Saddleworth.

light. The mullions serving as pilasters are rectangular in section and plain, and support a very simple entablature which is repeated over the two entrances in the west front. The nave is lit by a double row of four arched windows with simple 'Y' tracery on the north and south, with three on the west front. The treatment of the building is severely plain.

St. Anne's, Lydgate, has been virtually rebuilt this century, but Holy Trinity, Dobcross, remains substantially as built apart from an Italianate west tower, including entrance lobbies, added in 1843. It is larger than St. Thomas's but designed and built on the same principles, only the detailing is superior, especially in the design of the east window. Unlike St. Thomas's the windows do not have any tracery – and probably never did – both upper and lower windows being linked by a plain string course running round the building at the height of the spring of the arch to each window. There is a moulded cornice and the quoins stand proud of the face of the building.

It is on the quoins and window architraves that a distinctive change in building traditions is to be noted. This is the decorative effect of 'tooling' on the surface, a series of shallow parallel grooves across the face of the stone. This practice may have been evolved from the way a mason achieved a smooth finish to the outer surface of a walling stone by the use of a boaster. This is a broad chisel used for removing the rough surface from the stone which had already been roughly cut to rectangular faces at the quarry by means of a hammer or axe. Following the use of the boaster, normally on site, other specialist chisels would prepare the surface for a final rubbing with another stone to produce a smooth surface known as 'ashlar'. The textured treatment given to the stone by the boaster had been introduced to 'polite' architecture in the 1760's in those areas where carboniferous sandstones were the main building materials. This treatment is referred to as reeding and where the grooves are very close together (four or five to the inch) as corduroy work.[77] In Saddleworth it is reeded.

At Holy Trinity this effect is very noticeable on the quoins and window architraves, in the case of the former the effect is enhanced by drafted margins. This is where the grooves are cut at right-angles to the edges of the stone to the width of the boaster. The effect is very pleasing and adds a delicacy to the building. The architraves to the windows carry reeded tooling from edge to edge, but the sills have narrow drafted margins at the edges.

Such a practice would cost time and money, more so if the stone was the hard local gritstone. But here at Holy Trinity, the softer sandstones were used and over the last two hundred years the surfaces of the quoins and architraves have begun to spall, through the action of rain and frost.

The Venetian windows of the three churches found no immediate echo in the domestic architecture of the township, but classicism in a more subtle form was already making its way into the area in the shape of simple tripartite windows. These had first appeared at Woods House in Dobcross, built by John Harrop in 1782, where the central light is taller than its companions on either side, its lintel being supported by the lintels of the side lights. This is a variant of the stepped-lights familiar in the Pennines from the late seventeenth century when they are usually placed within the gable of a house. But at Woods House the windows are spaced symmetrically on the well-proportioned three-storey house which has a centrally placed entrance with a single-light Georgian sash window on each floor above; these windows are the same proportion as the central light of the tripartite windows. The front wall is capped with a well-moulded cornice, channelled for a rain gutter and with a decorative lead rainwater head initialled and dated JH 1782. Clearly a house of superior quality in Saddleworth and an expression of the increasing wealth being generated in Saddleworth by industry and commerce.

It is interesting to note that at Harrop Court, another three-storey building with a central doorway, the mullion windows were partially filled in so that they present a uniform

Harrop Court, Diggle. View from the south.

The Shaws, Uppermill. View of the rear. The smaller three-light window and masonry to the right are the remains of an early eighteenth century building.

The Shaws, Uppermill. From the left are numbers 6, 4, 3 and 2, the last two originally being one loomhouse. Note the two three-light windows on the right with the wider central lights for sash windows.

arrangement of three-light windows.

Both the tripartite window and the decorative tooling described above can be found at The Shaws, above Uppermill. As with most loomshop complexes, The Shaws has its origins in the early eighteenth century and part of the rear wall of number 3, which includes a three-light window, survives from that time. The present complex of buildings comprises six houses, but numbers 2 and 3 were formerly one large two-bay loomshop with a taking-in door at the rear on the first floor. The entrance front of this building which faces south-west, had the doorway centrally placed, a break in tradition, with four and five-light windows on the ground and first floor respectively to the left of the door and to the right a three-light window on each floor. The top (second) floor has a fourteen-light window both back and front with two-light cross-light windows in the south gable.

The two three-light windows mentioned above are different from the traditional form. First, the mullions are flush with the wall surface instead of being recessed; secondly, the central light is wider than those adjoining, not unlike the example at Oakdene Cottage described earlier. But here at The Shaws, the proportions of the centre light are similar to the shape of sash windows of the later Georgian period and did once house a vertical sash window. The rooms they illuminate contain the fireplaces and can be considered to have been the 'best' rooms, that is the housepart and the chamber over.

At The Shaws the quoins on the south-west and east corners have been given the same decorative treatment as those at Holy Trinity, Dobcross. Here they are as crisp as when cut and put into position at the turn of the century because these quoins are made from the tough millstone grit as also are the walls and windows, though the latter show no tooling except for a now blocked doorway at the rear of number 4.

Classicism was not confined to the better quality manufacturers' houses; it also appeared in the growing range of commercial buildings appearing in Saddleworth at this period, notably in the public houses being built along the new turnpike roads. The Stockport to Doctor Lane Head Turnpike of 1765 by-passed the fold at Lydgate. The Buckleys of Lydgate, who were already calling themselves innkeepers, realising that there was little scope for enlarging their old premises to accommodate the increasing trade, acquired land on the new turnpike and there built a new inn known as the White Hart in 1789.[78]

The front elevation of this three-storey building presents a new feature in the architectural scene of Saddleworth at this time, paired Georgian windows. Examples of these were to be found in Manchester in the 1780's but few now remain, and further afield they are still to be found on Standishgate in Wigan, on buildings dating from the 1770's.

Here at Lydgate the proportions are provincial Georgian; a cube and a third rather than a cube and a half in proportion, and quite typical for the region. The soffit of each lintel on the front of the White Hart is tooled in addition to the faces of the lintels, jambs and sills, and the same treatment is given to the centrally placed doorway. This too is given special treatment, the jambs becoming a formal arrangement of long and short stones of equal depth in the fashion of a simplified 'Gibbs' doorway with rusticated architrave. Here, instead of each of the longer stones projecting forward by half an inch over the intervening shorter stones, all the blocks of stone are flush with the wall of the building.

Further improvements were made to communications through Saddleworth by the Turnpike Act of 1792 providing an alternative route from Oldham to Standedge via Lydgate and Uppermill. By 1795, a new section of the Wakefield–Austerlands Road had been completed, by-passing Delph, and giving rise to New Delph where a new coaching inn was built. In 1797 a vestry meeting of St. Chads, Saddleworth was convened to be held 'at the House of William Bell, the New Inn, in New Delph'. This inn, now known as the Bell Inn, could then have only been recently built. Owing to its important position

Number 2 The Shaws, Uppermill. Tooling on the quoins at the south-west corner.

The White Hart, Lydgate. The west front.

The Bell Inn, New Delph. The elegant east front.

on the new turnpike road it was given an imposing architectural design incorporating elements of the current neo-classical architectural style; elegant, simple proportions, a symmetrical front, Georgian windows and a central doorway with pilasters and a pediment incorporating a fanlight. The architectural detailing is excellent with oval patera on the frieze supported by the Doric pilasters. This design was no doubt inspired by one or more of the numerous builder's pattern books of that time.[79] In spite of the classical details, the building retains local building traditions, especially in the use of water-shot masonry on all external walls.

In common with the White Hart at Lydgate, the Bell Inn incorporated paired Georgian windows on the front façade, those on the top floor being shorter in the typical Georgian and Regency fashion of the time. Significantly, the proportions of these windows on the Bell Inn are markedly superior to those on the White Hart.

A few years later and after 1800, James Lees, a Manchester cotton spinner, built Delph Lodge, across the turnpike road from the Bell Inn. This is the first 'grand' house to be built in Saddleworth. Five bays wide over a cellar, with a well-proportioned frontage graced with single Georgian sash windows and a central door clearly based on that at the Bell Inn, though not as well-proportioned. The whole building carried a good moulded cornice with a stub parapet. From the point of view of architectural excellence it was preceded by number 70 Denshaw Road, Linfitts, Delph.

Returning to the larger Saddleworth house represented by Woods House and the White Hart Inn, two further examples are worthy of notice. Cherry Clough House off Rochdale Road, Denshaw, was added by Joseph Gartside to an earlier house which still remains, although much altered. The new house is an imposing structure, three storeys high, three bays wide, with paired Georgian windows in the outer bays and single windows in the centre bay over the entrance. The sills to all the windows extend to form a continuous string course across the front of the building. The doorway has monolithic jambs which are finely moulded, the moulding being continued on the lintel. Above this is a blank frieze and then a cornice with classical moulding which is echoed by the cornice at the eaves, a handsome composition. The plan is double-pile with a vaulted cellar under the west end of the house.

From the front, Cherry Clough House gives the appearance of being a quietly prosperous gentleman's house, but round the corner of the west gable and at the far corner is a taking-in door at first floor level, reached by a flight of stone stairs. Inside and facing the door is a staircase leading up to the upper floor which is entirely open as if for a loomshop. Unlike examples of loomshops described so far, there are no multiples of mullion lights to form the familiar 'weaver's windows'. At the front are the two paired windows flanking the single Georgian window. In the rear are three Georgian windows with fixed frames on this upper floor. On the ground and first floor, Georgian windows flank a tall central staircase window lighting the main staircase leading up from the entrance to the first floor above. The three upper windows still retain their glazing which consists of thirty, small panes of glass and the windows on the front would have once been glazed in the same way, but with vertical sliding sashes for ventilation.

In the east gable is a small fireplace presumably to help maintain temperature rather than heat the space. The west gable has collapsed, so it is not known if there was another small fireplace at that end. Two queen trusses support the roof, the queen posts being secured to the tiebeam by iron brackets bolted to the timbers. The trusses carry three purlins per pitch. The tiebeams here show some very fine examples of the Baltic consignment marks. There is no sign of a hoist, the taking-in door is of normal size, the rear staircase is of the standard width of 27 inches, so the use of this upper room as a warehouse does not seem feasible, but on the other hand, its use as a loomshop is not entirely convincing.

The Bell Inn, New Delph. The entrance
doorway showing the neo-classical
architectural features of pediment, frieze and
pilasters.

Delph Lodge, New Delph.

Delph Lodge, New Delph. View from the south.

Cherry Clough House, Rochdale Road, Denshaw. The south front.

Warehouse?

Kitchen

Pantry

Cellar

Housepart

Parlour

0 5 10 feet

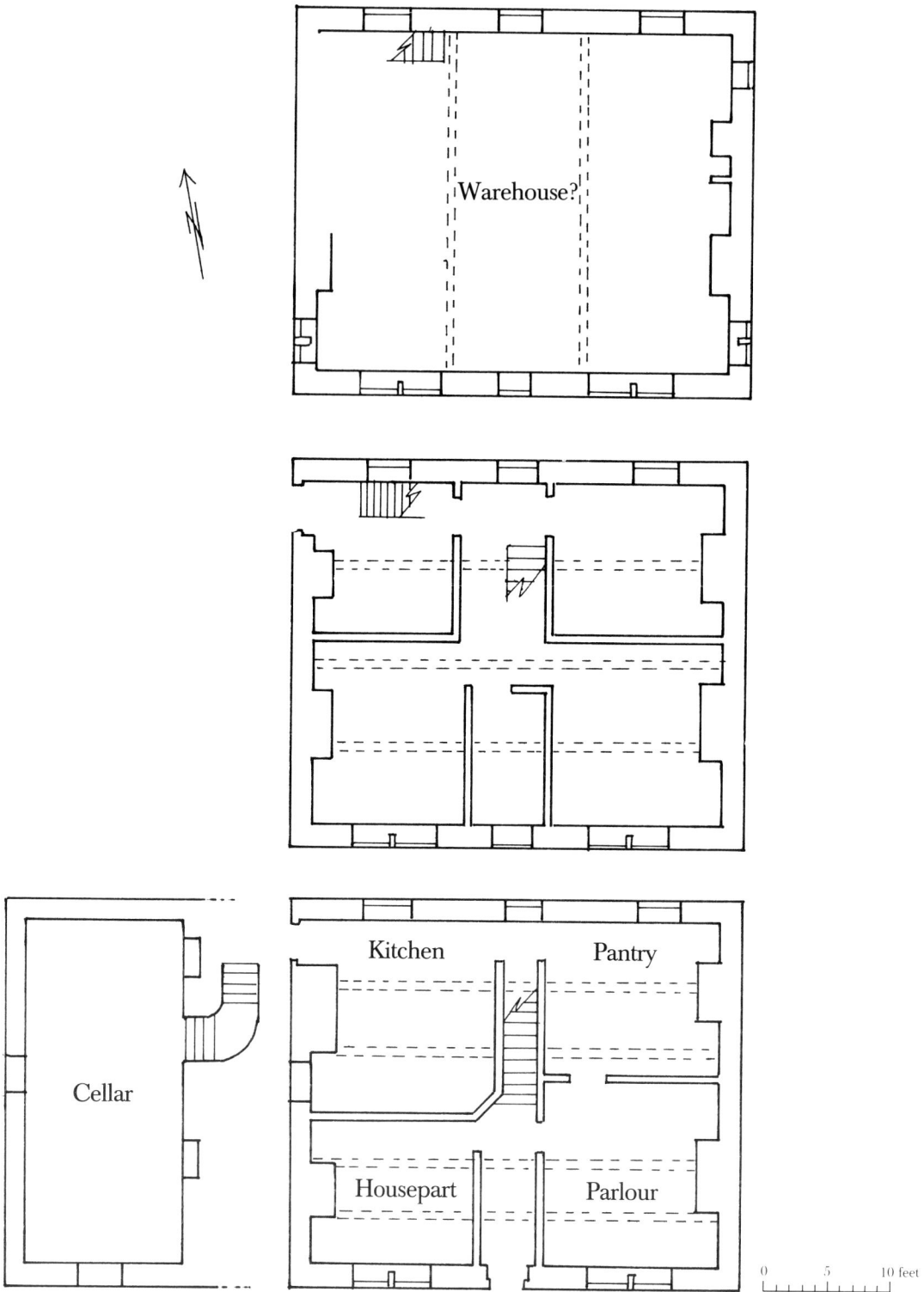

Cherry Clough House, Rochdale Road, Denshaw. Plan of the three floors.

A similar building but of only two storeys, is number 72 Church Road, opposite Saddleworth Fold, Uppermill. At the rear are three-light mullion windows and a tall staircase window in the centre, but no sign of a taking-in door. Presumably this house was for domestic use only. This house and Cherry Clough House were built shortly before 1822 – both are featured on the Township Map of the date. To the south at the Junction, Denshaw, is the building now occupied by the Denshaw Oddfellows Club. The building is of two storeys and in general the design of the front follows that of the previous examples, but the entrance door here is more elaborate. The door has rusticated jambs carrying a monolithic lintel made to look as if it had been built from voussoirs with a bold keystone in the centre. On this keystone is cut the date '1818'. Above the voussoirs is a flat hood or cornice, with a classical moulding. A similar doorway is at the rear of the block of houses opposite and another, now blocked, is to be seen on the White Lion Inn in Delph, and both are presumably of the same date.

During the first two decades of the nineteenth century, the character of the landscape was changing with many of these larger and architecturally more sophisticated houses appearing in the countryside, often with older property alongside or close by, a clear indication of commercial success bringing greater wealth to the area.

Mills

The mill buildings and factories which are a distinctive feature of the landscape are not featured in this Guide, with the exception of two, both in Delph.[80]

Shore Mill on the south bank of the river Tame and just out of the centre of Delph, was built circa 1782[81] as a scribbling mill, but by 1788 it was spinning cotton. Power was provided by a water wheel, five feet in diameter, the water being taken from the river Tame near Delph Bridge.

The essential characteristics of the eighteenth century loomshops are seen here in the long ranges of mullion lights and taking-in door in the north gable. There were two entrances on the east front and both are wider than those on domestic housing of this period, they are now blocked. There were no internal divisions except for a period when a house was incorporated within it for a time.[82]

Hull Mill standing close by the Hull Brook to the north of Delph, was built circa 1787[83] for cotton spinning. It is three storeys, but larger than Shore Mill. The mullion windows have three-lights and are arranged symmetrically. At one corner are taking-in doors at each floor level. In recent years it has been heightened and enlarged in brick.

Both mills clearly show their origins in the local vernacular traditions, but with Hull Mill moving more towards the familiar cotton spinning mill image.

Shore Mill, Delph. The vernacular characteristics are still very much in evidence.

Hull Mill, Delph. Showing a more formal arrangement of three-light mullion windows.

Chapter 6.   The Spread of Classicism in Saddleworth

Not all the superior houses of Saddleworth were the product of commercial success. Some wealth was acquired by other means. The descendants of the Buckley family of New Tame appear to have married wisely and well from the late seventeenth century, and to have established themselves in other parts of Saddleworth. One branch settled at Linfitts, near Delph, in the 1680's when John Buckley and his wife Alice built a house there. Only the datestone now survives with their initials and date JB AB 1685. The male members of this family are styled 'gentlemen' in the late eighteenth century, an indication that they held a status separate from that of a clothier and perhaps socially superior.[84] Number 70 Denshaw Road, Linfitts, was built in 1793 by either James Buckley (died 1807) or his son John (died 1810), descendants of John and Alice Buckley. The wives of both James and John were called Elizabeth and on the rainwater head are the initials and date JBB 1793, the last 'B' is no doubt for Betty the diminutive for Elizabeth. Both father and son are described as of Linfitts and styled 'gentleman' up to 1807, so it is far from clear which of them built the house, but this problem does not detract from what was built. This house is the earliest domestic building in Saddleworth to show a strong influence of 'polite' architecture in its total composition as well as in the style of architectural details. The quality of design is equalled by the quality of detail and construction.

The front façade is symmetrical, three bays wide with a central doorway in a good Gibbsian style, and five sash windows with good moulded architraves. The walling rises from a narrow reeded plinth with a quarter round moulding on top, the walling is of narrow coursed stones, three inches deep and laid in water-shot coursing. A bold plain string course runs across the front just above the ground floor window lintels. At the eaves is a well-moulded cornice with lintels which break forward slightly at each end, a quiet subtlety which enriches the overall design. Well cut quoins with evidence of tooling complete the composition. On the front elevation the architectural details, except the plinth, are painted white, and have been for a long time. However, the rear of the building presents quite a different picture, for there the vernacular remains, not a sign of classicism, instead four windows of mullion lights give illumination to the rooms at the rear.

The plan is double-pile with a central passage which contains the staircase. Just inside the door are entrances leading into the two principal rooms on the ground floor, each fifteen feet square and proportionally high. The passage leads through to a long kitchen with a large fireplace and beyond, a pantry.

The rooms on the first floor follow the same plan, but the room over the kitchen once had a separate means of access by a stone staircase outside the building. So this upper room once had a special function, but it is doubtful that it was ever weaving, as there is only one four-light window and the room is long.

Without doubt, the most exiting feature of the house is its front entrance. In national terms it is old-fashioned for its day, and the design must have come from a pattern book of half a century earlier, but for Saddleworth it was new, different and definitely superior.

The Gibbsian door surround is rusticated with a pulvinated frieze and a heavy keystone capped by a pediment. This type was popularised by James Gibbs through his very successful 'A Book of Architecture' published in 1728 and later by his equally successful 'Rules for Drawing the Several Parts of Architecture' which appeared in 1732 with a second edition in 1738.[85] Other architects of lesser fame, builders, craftsmen and publishers, issued a vast number of similar pattern books or handbooks during the eighteenth century frequently 'borrowing' plates from each other.

At 70 Denshaw Road, Linfitts, the intermittent blocks of rustication break the moulded architrave of the door and the pulvinated frieze is interrupted by four large voussoirs and a heavy keystone which breaks through the pediment. It is identical to the west and east

Number 72 Church Road, Uppermill. South front.

Number 72 Church Road, Uppermill. Gable end and rear, showing the deep narrow staircase window.

Denshaw Oddfellows Club, dated 1818 on the keystone over the door.

Denshaw Oddfellows Club. Entrance
doorway with rusticated jambs and lintel
with moulded cornice.

The White Lion Inn, Delph Lane, Delph.
The original entrance which is similar to that
at the Denshaw Oddfellows Club.

Number 70 Denshaw Road, Linfitts. The west front.

Number 70 Denshaw Road, Linfitts. The rainwater head and detail of the cornice. The initials and date are damaged but it was recorded by J. Radcliffe last century.

doors to St. Martins-in-the-Fields, London, designed by Gibbs and built 1722–26 and featured in *'A Book of Architecture'*.

In the introduction to *'Rules for Drawing'*, Gibbs explains how he has simplified the calculations for drawing the designs of doorcases, windows, cornices and other features, by the use of simple division

> ". . . which will be found so beneficial to workmen in drawing any part at large . . . that when they are at once accustom'd to it, they will never follow any other".

A sentiment echoed by other compilers of pattern books.

It is not surprising, therefore, to meet up with this splendid example of 'polite' architecture of the 1790's in a small Pennine parish. But it is not alone. Facing onto Church Fields in Dobcross is the Manor House, built by Joseph Lawton a clothier, soon after he had purchased the land in 1804.[86] Included in this purchase were ten shares in the Manor of Saddleworth which then entitled Joseph Lawton to become one of the Lords of the Manor of Saddleworth and, not surprisingly, his house became known as the Manor House – one of several in Saddleworth renamed at this time.

The north front shows the same arrangement of paired sash windows, rusticated doorway, string course at first floor level and a moulded cornice at the eaves. There are sash windows in the gable ends and small arched lights in the apex of each gable, but the surprise is at the rear. Here, in what was a rear extension giving the house a 'T' plan, is a most remarkable architectural feature in Saddleworth – or anywhere else in the region – a large Venetian window with rusticated surrounds in the best Gibbsian manner, and topped by a pediment extending the full width of the wing. A first response is to think of it as being intended for the east window of a church, but no church or chapel of that date has similar architectural details. Clearly it is a further example of pattern book influence.

Its purpose would have been two-fold, first to give light for a staircase and secondly to present an imposing architectural feature to travellers and visitors ascending Woods Lane, and from the position of the building on its high elevation it would have been seen from a wide area south of Dobcross. (Later houses now get in the way.) Sometime after 1820 the angles on either side of this wing were built up, providing two small domestic units in one of which a private day-school was run for many years.

Naturally there were other imitations of this Gibbsian style. At Roughtown in Mossley is a fine provincial interpretation of the doorway at Linfitts, it is a simplified version with rustication but no moulded architraves and with a lintel carved with bold voussoirs and a pediment over it. This rusticated surround to a doorway, with the appropriate lintel, became very popular from the 1830's for the next forty years and can be seen on a great many houses, especially terrace houses, in Oldham and Saddleworth. So many in fact that there must have been a builder's or mason's yard in the district producing these jambs and lintels. There are a good range of these doorways to be seen in Austerlands and Lees. A few lintels are dated on the keystone, one is now preserved at the Oldham Local Interest Centre and this has the initials and date J^{K}A 1837 beautifully cut into the stone. Most keystones were however, decorated with carving, the most common being a form of fluting giving the impression of folded cloth. The earliest dated example of this type of decoration was on the former Independent Methodist Sunday School on George Street, Oldham, dated 1832.

A lintel identical to the dated example given above, is on the new front to Hill End, Delph. This house began as a typical two-unit plan of the mid-eighteenth century with a gable entrance. In the 1830's it was given a new front with a central doorway and the interior was altered. Paired sash windows to either side of the door on each floor and a single sash window over the door were provided. The front was completed with a moulded cornice topped with a shallow parapet. This front was also extended east by one bay and a wing added to the rear at the west end.

Number 70 Denshaw Road, Linfitts. Ground floor window showing the moulded architrave.

Number 70 Denshaw Road, Linfitts. Plinth showing the reeded decoration. The quoins also have decorative tooling, but it is largely obscured with white paint.

Number 70 Denshaw Road, Linfitts. Rear view. The right-hand wing is a later addition.

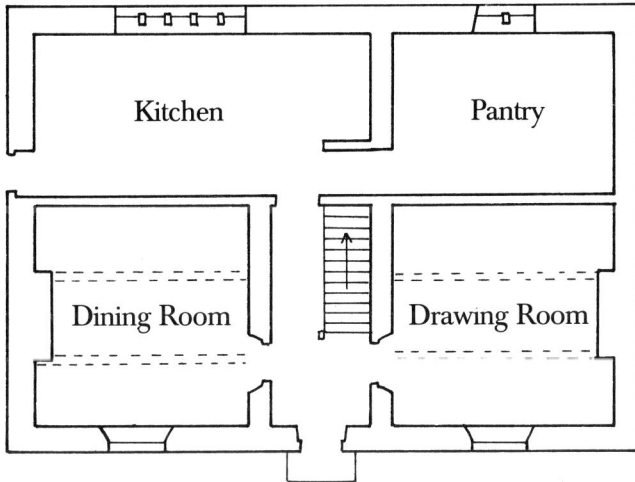

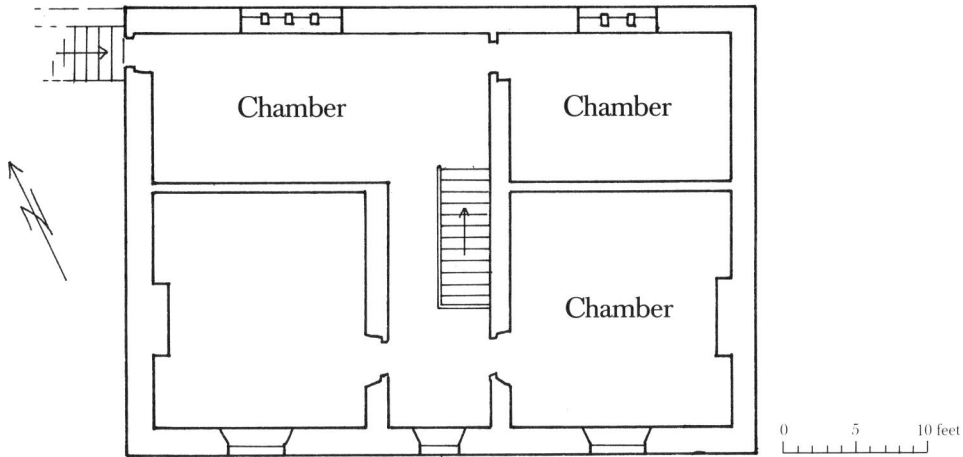

Number 70 Denshaw Road, Linfitts. Front elevation and plan plan of ground and first floor.

The Manor House, Dobcross. The front facing north onto Church Fields.

Number 70 Denshaw Road, Linfitts. The 'Gibbsian' door.

The Manor House, Dobcross. The rear wing showing the 'Gibbsian' Venetian window and pediment. The rainwater gutter disturbs the design. The doorway beneath is modern.

At Carr House on Standedge Road (the A670) this form of decorative door case is used on both the entrance and the taking-in door above on the upper floor, but both with plain keystones. This section of road was the result of a Turnpike Act passed in 1827, authorising new branch roads on the Oldham–Standedge Turnpike. The branch from Wool Road via Bleak Hey Nook to Standedge is supposed to have been completed within twelve months of the Act,[87] so it would be soon after 1828 that Carr House was built. It stands against the embankment of the new road with the ground floor being below the level of the road and facing east, and with the two upper floors adjacent to the road. Hence the decorative door cases facing onto the new turnpike road. The examples to be seen at Austerlands and Lees also stand alongside the turnpike roads and must have conveyed the appearance of relative prosperity to travellers of the 1830's.

Roughtown, Mossley. A simplified version of the Gibb's style.

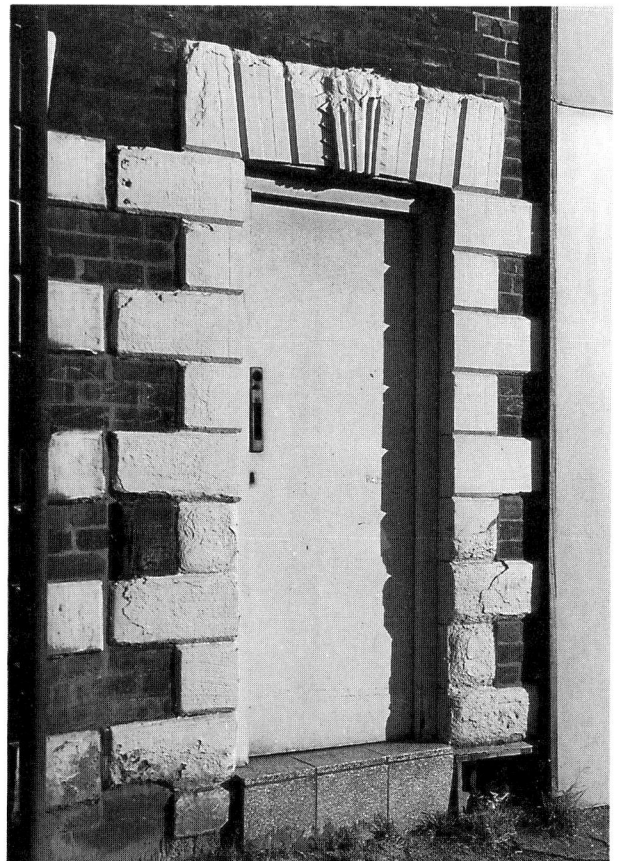

Adjoining doorways on Huddersfield Road, Oldham. The terrace has been demolished but a dated lintel is preserved.

Hill End, Delph. View from the west. The central doorway is very similar to that on Huddersfield Road. The original gable entrance is blocked.

Carr House, Standedge Road. The entrance door and taking-in door, both having the same decorative treatment, in this case with plain keystones.

Carr House, Standedge Road. The west front.

Church Fields, Dobcross. Byre door at former barn, dated 1748.

Smithy Lane, Uppermill. Farmhouse remaining from the former fold at Uppermill.

Numbers 7 to 11 High Street, Delph. They form a very picturesque view.

Chapter 7.   Some Urban Developments

Up to the end of the eighteenth century there were no villages in Saddleworth, only 'folds', small groups of buildings mainly farm houses, loomshops and barns, but some of these folds developed, partly through their geographical position the growth of trade and the interests of developers, into the villages of Delph, Dobcross and Uppermill.

All owe much of their rise to being on important routes through Saddleworth. Dobcross and Uppermill grew up where routes converged or crossed, and Delph where there was a river crossing over the Tame, firstly by a ford and later by a bridge. The ford crossed at the confluence of the River Tame and the Hull Brook where silt and gravel were deposited so making a shallow crossing. The line of the approach to the ford is still clear.

At Dobcross and Uppermill, the remains of former farmhouses and barns of the original fold are still to be seen near the road junctions. The remains of a barn dated 1748 are just north of Church Fields in Dobcross, the left jamb of the former barn door remains and the width of the surviving (dated) door suggests its former use as a byre door. On Sandy Lane is a barn of the earlier eighteenth century later converted into a house and now known as Briarfield Cottage, and on Platt Lane is Platt Lane Farm dated 1726 which also incorporates a barn and byre.

In Uppermill a former barn is behind the Conservative Club. It is now a short terrace of later nineteenth century houses – but look at the east gable end. Barns can have later windows and doorways built in and be divided into rooms, but often as a measure of economy, the former ventilation slots (larp holes) are merely filled in leaving their outline clear and unmistakable as can also be seen at Briarfield Cottage.

The house at the junction of High Street, Uppermill, (a Turnpike road of 1792) and Smithy Lane, is a former farmhouse. It was once part of the fold at Uppermill, and lay alongside the old route from west to east across the Tame valley. This came via Burnedge Lane and Dry Clough Lane to Dark Lane and then up Smithy Lane, Church Road and Hay Lane to the junction with Gellfield Lane and on to Pob Green.

The houses comprising the fold at Delph were demolished around 1950. Their site is now the car park for the White Lion Inn, but before this pub was built they stood beside the 'Great Way' which preceded the Wakefield to Austerlands Turnpike.

Alongside the road leading down to the ford at Delph were built two cottages in 1769. When the bridge was built in the 1770's the road was realigned to the east and so these cottages and adjoining buildings – including an inn – were to remain at an angle to the new road. Further, as the route became used more and more by wheeled traffic, it was heightened and levelled to form a causeway. The buildings to the south of this bridge are now below the present road level, and the bridge parapets had to be heightened to meet the new road level.

From its beginnings by the ford and bridge, Delph developed along King Street and High Street (north of the river) and later along what is now known as Millgate. Just north of the river is a curious and picturesque grouping of numbers 7–11 High Street, this site was dictated by the piece of land left between the old road leading up from the ford and the later turnpike road leading through Delph after it had passed over the bridge on its way north of Delph Hill and on to Standedge.

Architecturally and socially, the most significant buildings are the shops along High Street, King Street and Millgate. Many of these survive on the east side of the road, most have two large shop windows on either side of the entrance. These windows were originally multi-paned and a photograph taken early in this century shows each window to have contained as many as twenty panes with very fine glazing bars.

The window sills of numbers 2 and 4 Millgate, and 14, 16 and 18 King Street are set low down, whereas numbers 6 and 8 Millgate, and 12 and 18 King Street have stone panels

Number 2 Millgate, Delph. Two former shops, dating from the 1830's. They were a refronting of an earlier building.

Rear of number 2 Millgate, Delph, showing the earlier structure.

Numbers 8 and 6 Millgate, Delph.

Number 8 King Street, Delph. A fine Regency shop front complete with contemporary railings.

Number 8 King Street, Delph. Detail of shop front and railing.

Number 8 Millgate, Delph.

Lawton Square, Delph. Coach house, perhaps converted from a barn.

Lawton Square, Delph. Rear of coach house, the blocked doorway could have been meant for a threshing door.

beneath the windows supported on a plinth and framed by the plain pilaster to the windows, a feature which gives the façades a more pleasing sense of design and proportion.

Similar examples are to be found elsewhere, for instance there are at least three in Crawshawbooth, Rossendale and two or more in Lees, near Oldham.

It is worth drawing attention to the design of shop fronts appearing in London at this time,[88] in basic principles the same, but being larger and having a little more refinement in architectural style and decoration, for instance, in the treatment of the pilasters flanking the shop windows and the carved moulding above the lintels.

In some respects Saddleworth may have been behind the mainstream of architectural design, but in its shops it was up-to-date, and nowhere more so than at number 8 King Street, Delph. Here is a double-fronted shop combining windows and entrance but the windows are delicately bowed, supported on a plain stone sill that follows the curve and capped by a simple but gracefully moulded cornice in stone, details typical of the early nineteenth century.

The shop stands above the street level and a short flight of steps gives access to a balcony running the full length of the shop. The original railings survive; they include two gates, one at the top of the steps and the other opposite to the shop door, thus enabling loading and unloading to be carried out from the cart or horse at a convenient level. The main supports to the railings have small urns as finials while the railings end in a flat pointed shape.

Beneath the shop are cellars with access from under the balcony. There was once a similar shop opposite, but this and its companions were demolished to make way for a new row of shops with housing above in the late nineteenth century.[89] Fashionable number 8 may have been, but the upper floor still retained the local tradition of mullion windows.

Number 8 Millgate is the tallest of the Delph shops. From a basement storey it rises through four floors, having mullion windows to the rear but sash windows on the gable end and the front façade. Here is the usual double-fronted shop front of the type already described, but to the south are three full height taking-in doors, one above the other, and on the top floor are the remains of a hoist. At eaves level the cornice is supported by a pulvinated frieze completing a dignified composition. For much of its earlier life it was the shop of a corn chandler and grocer.

In addition to the shops there were once several inns of which only four now survive, they are the White Lion, Rose and Crown, Swan and Bulls Head. Increasing trade from and through Saddleworth encouraged the number of inns and coaching houses with their attendant outhouses. In Lawton Square, behind King Street, is a large building that could easily be mistaken for a barn with its high arched doorway. In this respect it is similar to a barn on Lawton Square which backs on to Shore Mill leat. (The front of this barn is severely disfigured but sufficient remains to reveal its original design.) What appears to be a barn is a coach house with stables, tack room and lodgings for grooms and ostlers. That this building was intended to be longer is evidenced by the tuskings on the north gable end. Perhaps when the new turnpike road by-passing Delph was opened in 1795, the through passage trade declined and so this building remained unfinished.

Uppermill came into its own with the opening of the Turnpike road in 1794, and from the nucleus of the old fold lying on the higher land north of the river Tame, it gradually spread north and south along High Street. At the turn of the century New Street was added as an easier and wider route to St. Chads Church and the old track along Gellfield Lane. Smithy Lane was constricted at this time (and still is) by the building already referred to earlier and the corn mill with its mill pond immediately to the south.

Numbers 1–13 New Street were built in three stages within the first two decades of the nineteenth century and represented a row of superior housing. Each house is of three

Numbers 9, 11 and 13 New Street, Uppermill.

Rear of numbers 11 and 13 New Street, Uppermill.

storeys, and has an entrance with plain rusticated surrounds and single sash window above on each floor. The main rooms have three-light tripartite windows very similar to those in number 2 The Shaws, which is not very far away. The mullions are flush with the outer wall. It is a handsome terrace. At the rear however, each house is seen to have loomshops on the upper two floors with external access via taking-in doors at first floor level – now mostly blocked. These were reached by steps, one set of which survives behind number 3.

Shortly after 1822 the row was extended by a two-bay building, number 15. Here are sash windows to each floor, a single sash and two paired sash windows on each of the two upper floors. The walls are of flush coursing laid with very fine joints – unlike its neighbours. At the eaves is a bold, moulded stone cornice, which ends at each corner. On the ground floor is the architectural gem, a double-fronted shop façade similar to number 8 King Street, Delph, but here the windows and door are given the full architectural treatment. Both windows are bowed with a plain sill, but the lintel, which continues over the door, has a pulvinated frieze with a moulded cornice over, which has a cyma recta section. The windows are framed by plain jambs, but the door jambs are decorated with a recessed panel which has a convex face. The jamb rises from a square base and finishes with an appropriate classical capital. The lintel has a segmental arch with curved panels with the same section as on the jambs, on either side of a keystone. In each spandrel is a well-cut oval patera. Above the door is a segmental fanlight with radial glazing bars supporting a scalloped edging.

The whole composition is one of great refinement, but, alas, to achieve this quality of design the stone used was not laid on its bed, but turned through ninety degrees to present a smooth surface for carving. The result now is that the carved surface is breaking away from the stone through the action of rain and frost. To the left of the shop front is a quietly elegant door leading into the private part of the building. The lintel is decorated by a keystone similar to that over the shop door, and the surface is tooled, as are the rusticated jambs. As with the other houses in the row, the rear presents a totally different character with seven-light mullion windows on the first and second floors, both of which have taking-in doors, and on the ground floor is a four-light window alongside the rear door. At the eaves the gutters are carried on projecting plain, stone brackets, a feature that continues all down the row.

Number 6 Court Street, Uppermill, a three-bay three-storey building, may also have been a shop. To the right on the central doorway is a shallow bay with a low sill and moulded lintel similar to those described above, except that it is not bowed but is angled. The two floors above each have three sash windows but at the rear, not surprisingly, are mullion windows and a taking-in door at first floor level, reached by a stone staircase.

Across High Street, from New Street, a row of loomhouses were built about 1800. This group of buildings known as St. Mary's Gate, includes at its north east end where the ground rises, the 'Manor House' built by John Buckley around the turn of the nineteenth century. It follows the pattern for this date seen elsewhere in Saddleworth, of paired and single sash windows and a door with a classical architrave. At the rear in an extension, is an arched staircase window, framed by the traditional mullion windows on either side. It is now the Conservative Club.

The southern part of this block, numbers 2 and 4 St. Mary's Gate, also have the double sash windows and plain rusticated door surrounds, the side of number 2 facing onto High Street (number 73 now the newsagents) once had a bow window shop front. Behind these two houses and sharing the same rear walls, are two loomhouses with the usual mullion windows.

With the development of communication and transport there had to be provision for horses, carts and waggons, as already seen at Delph. Number 3 School Street, off High

Number 15 New Street, Uppermill. Shop front with the private door to the left.

Number 15 New Street, Uppermill.

Number 15 New Street, Uppermill. View of the rear.

The Conservative Club, High Street, Uppermill. This was the 'Manor House' built by John Buckley. The square panels on the ends of ties put in to strengthen the walls.

Numbers 2 and 4 St. Mary's Gate, Uppermill. Note the ornate setting of the taking-in doors on number 4.

Numbers 3 and 5 School Street, Uppermill. The archway is now partially blocked by a later entrance into the house.

Numbers 3 and 5 School Street, Uppermill. Courtyard. Note the taking-in doors and remains of loading platform.

Street in Uppermill, built after 1822, has an archway leading through to the yard at the rear. This building was added between the rear of number 44 High Street, which appears on the 1822 Map just to the south of the river Tame, and number 5 School Street. This too was built after 1822 on the plot of land to the rear of 44 High Street; it has a gable entrance and recessed mullion windows on both floors. Built as a single-bay house, it was extended by a further bay which had flush mullion windows – all very traditional but becoming old-fashioned by the late 1820's.

Number 3 completed the development of the plot of land. It 'borrowed' the west side wall of number 5 and the rear of number 44 High Street, at which point it keyed in the segmental arch which is a principal feature extending to nearly half the frontage. On the upper floor are two paired sash windows the sills of which are extended to form a string course – a feature observed elsewhere. To the right of the arch are now two square windows, the left-hand one being original but that to the right was the doorway into this building. It was narrower than the present window and the foot of the door jambs are still visible below the sill – where they have been given false coursing. At the rear is an upper taking-in door with the remains of a stone platform. Alongside at the rear of number 5a are taking-in doors on both floors, all now blocked. Clearly the arch was to give access to the yard for the purpose of loading or unloading houses or waggons. The building may have been a small warehouse or counting house.

At Austerlands there is an archway, now blocked, in the row of buildings which includes the Three Crowns Inn built before 1822 on Huddersfield Road, and further west at 91 Huddersfield Road is a further example. Both are associated with domestic housing. At the Granby Arms in Uppermill, a flat arch leads into the yard behind where there were no doubt, stables for changing or refreshing horses.

Architecturally, the most sophisticated building of this period in Uppermill is the Commercial Inn in The Square, built by James Buckley, a banker, before 1828.[90] It is a three-bay building of two storeys and a cellar, and is two rooms deep. The front is of ashlar laid in regular courses with fine joints. The central doorway has jambs and lintel with a broad reeded moulding, with a square panel at their junction on which is carved a geometrical floral design. The lintel carries a stone panel on which is carved the emblems of a beer jug, two goblets and two tureen covers, all between two smaller panels decorated with a lozenge shape, over this panel is a moulded cornice.

Above the door is a tripartite window with slender pillars acting as mullions, the projecting sill being supported by two brackets. Paired sash windows are on each side of the entrance with single sash windows above. A moulded cornice with parapet completes the design. The features are not unlike those which appear at Holly Ville, Greenfield, the home of James Buckley, and the architect or builder could well have been the same person.

Each gable rises in a sweep to a pair of chimney stacks, the south gable having a blocked taking-in door over which is a lunette window, also blocked. Beneath is a long staircase window with a side entrance below, this has moulded architraves surmounted by a stone panel with decorative carving and over this, a moulded cornice.

There are few commercial buildings in Dobcross, two warehouses now much altered and two banks. These were the only banks in Saddleworth up to the 1830's. To the south of The Square where it meets Sugar Lane, is a row of two shops (one with altered windows) which were added to the row of pre 1822 buildings behind. Of these shops, one was built for the Saddleworth Union Bank founded by John Harrop around 1810, the premises were improved between 1822 and 1826 when the bank failed.[91] The lintels of door and windows are extended to form a deep string course while the sills of the windows above extend to form a narrower string course. As is usual at this period the front elevation is completed by a moulded cornice acting as a rainwater gutter.

The Commercial Inn, The Square, Uppermill.

Numbers 10 and 12 The Square, Dobcross.

On the east gable is a small Venetian window, a miniature of the one in the chancel of the Holy Trinity Church round the corner on Woods Lane. This east gable extension is at an angle to the earlier gable and this was to ensure an unimpeded access into the Square from Sugar Lane by carts and coaches.

Across the Square is another bank building, but less architecturally distinguished. This was the Saddleworth Bank opened by Buckley Roberts and Co. in 1813. This is a good example of "Queen Anne in front, Mary Ann behind" which typifies most of Saddleworth's Regency buildings.

Conclusion

This Guide ends in the 1840's when building traditions of centuries past were giving way to types and designs that owed little to the vernacular idiom of Saddleworth.

Hollyville on Holmfirth Road, built by James Buckley around 1820 and High Grove in Grasscroft, built by James Wright at about the same time, are indications of the new trends in architecture already seen in the commercial buildings of Delph, Dobcross and Uppermill, but there the new architectural forms were restricted to the 'business' parts, i.e. the shop fronts, the rear still showing the use of traditional features such as mullion windows.

Later in the 1850's, Scottish Baronial was to grace the landscape at Ashway Gap and a plethora of Victorian Gothic churches, villas, terraces and shops continued the growth of the villages, mercifully not dominating the landscape but acting as a foil to the local vernacular buildings. George Shaw led the way with the treatment of his classical fronted house, St. Chads, on High Street, Uppermill, turning it into a 'Tudorbethan' mansion.[92]

It is fortunate that Saddleworth has escaped the worst faults of 'development'. Restoration and renovation is often handled with some regard to the local character. Strap pointing is still the main cause for concern, but it will fall off and the walls should then be pointed in the proper way.[93]

Saddleworth has been well served by an active Historical Society the lectures and publications of which have done much to increase knowledge and appreciation of the historic buildings of the area. A vigilant Civic Trust and many enlightened individuals have helped to ensure that the architectural inheritance of this fascinating parish is being preserved for future generations.

The Saddleworth Bank, The Square, Dobcross.

The Saddleworth Bank, The Square, Dobcross. The rear.

St. Chad's, High Street, Uppermill. Refronted by George Shaw in the mid-nineteenth century.

Glossary

Architrave:	the classical designed surround to a window.
Ashlar:	square-cut, smooth-faced masonry.
Baffle:	See *Lobby*.
Baluster:	a short pillar, supporting the hand rail of a staircase.
Bay:	a constructional unit of a building, usually the space between roof trusses.
Brace:	an inclined timber inserted to lend strength to a structure.
Buttery:	an alternative name for Pantry.
Byre:	a cow house.
Castellated:	decorated with battlements.
Cavetto:	a concave hollow moulding, especially of mullions.
Chamber:	a bedroom.
Chamfer:	to cut away the square angle of a block of stone or piece of timber at an angle of 45 degrees.
Collar:	a tie-beam applied near the apex of the roof truss. (See page 14.)
Corbel:	a stone projecting from a wall to support an overhanging structure.
Course:	a continuous layer of stone.
Cross-lights:	supplementary windows in a gable end.
Cruck:	a large curved timber supporting the roof and walls of a building. (See page 14).
Daub:	walling material of clay or dung, mixed with grass or hair, plastered on to wattle.
Door case:	the frame or structure in which the door is hung.
Double fronted:	having windows either side of the door.
Double pile:	being two rooms in depth.
Dove tail joint:	(See page 14).
Dual houses:	a pair of houses built together with similar or identical façades.
Façade:	the main face or front of a building.
Finial:	a heavy, decorative stone at the apex of a gable or top of a pediment.
Gargoyle:	a water spout projecting from the parapet of a building, carved in the form of an animal or human mouth.
Gibbsian:	after the architect James Gibbs (1682–1754).
Half-lap joint:	(See page 15).
Hood mould:	a projecting moulding over a door or window lintel to divert rain water.
Inglenook:	(See page 29).
Italianate:	the architectural style based loosely on that of the Italian renaissance.
Jamb:	the side post of a door or window.
Keystone:	the stone at the apex of an arch locking the whole together.
King mullion:	a larger mullion extending the full thickness of a wall.

King post:	a vertical timber connecting the tie-beam with the apex of a roof truss.
Larp holes:	small ventilation holes in the wall of a barn.
Laithe:	a barn and byre combined in one structure.
Laithe house:	a house and byre under one roof with no internal communication.
Lath:	a thin strip of wood placed across the common rafters on which are hung the roofing flags.
Lintel:	a horizontal stone over a door or window opening.
Lobby:	the space created around a doorway by a baffle, speer or inner doorway.
Longhouse:	a house and barn under one roof with common entrance for humans and animals.
Lunette:	a semi-circular window.
Mullion:	a vertical post dividing a window into two or more lights.
Ogee:	a term used in gothic architecture to describe a double curve, convex turning to concave.
Parapet:	a decorative feature consisting of a low wall surmounting the façade of a building.
Patera:	a dish-shaped carving in relief.
Pediment:	a triangular feature used in classical architecture surmounting a façade or opening.
Plinth:	the projecting part of a wall immediately above ground level.
Purlin:	a horizontal timber joining gables and roof trusses. (See page 29).
Quoins:	large stones providing greater strength at the corner of a wall or opening and giving a decorative effect.
Rafter:	inclined timbers supported by purlins, forming the side of a roof. (See page 29.)
Rainwater head:	an iron or lead casting which collects water from a gutter in order to convey it down a drain pipe.
Roof truss:	the entire assembly of timbers supporting a roof. (See page 29).
Rustication:	the deliberate emphasis of the joints between stones, often achieved by chamfering the edges of the face of each stone.
Shoulder stop:	the point at which a chamfer meets a square section.
Spalling:	the splitting of stone along the bedding plane by the action of the weather.
Spandrel:	the space created at the angle of an arch and a hood mould.
Smoke hood:	a structure designed to take smoke from the inglenook to the chimney, usually constructed of wattle and daub. (See page 29).
Spere:	the partition protecting the inglenook from the entrance doorway. (See page 29).
String course:	a horizontal moulding or projection across the façade of a building.
Stylobate:	in vernacular architecture, the stone on which a cruck blade rests. (See page 14).

Threshing door:	a small door opposite the main entrance to a barn creating a draught to assist winnowing.
Taking-in door:	an exterior door giving access to a loomshop. Sometimes a hoist was provided but in other cases the door was reached via a flight of steps.
Tie-beam:	the timber at the base of a roof truss. (See page 29).
Tracery:	decorative stonework separating lights at the top of a window.
Tuskings:	stones left projecting where it was intended to continue the line of building.
Venetian window:	a three-light window with the central light terminating in a semi-circular arch.
Voussoirs:	wedge-shaped stones used in the composition of an arch.
Wattle:	an interwoven framework of laths or branches on to which daub was plastered.
Wall plate:	the horizontal timber at the top of a wall on which the base of the rafters rest. (See page 14).
Yoke:	a horizontal timber joining cruck blades at the apex. (See page 14).

Footnotes

1   A. Wrigley. (1931), p.35.

2   Geological Survey of Great Britain. (1933).

3   R. Muir. (1986). pp.43–47.

4   *British Journal.* January 4th, 1766.

5   *Commercial Directory.* (1817).

6   J. Radcliffe. (1887). pp.465–469.

7   J. Aikin. (1795). p.557.

8   B. Barnes. (1981). pp.5–19.

9   J. Bottomley. (1816). Frontispiece.

10 A. J. Howcroft. (1923). pp.1–10.

11 Raines Mss Vol.8 fol.232. Chetham's Library, Manchester.

12 A. N. Alcock. (1981). pp.2–27.

13 See Glossary for this and other technical terms which follow.

14 *Wills and Inventories. Vol.I.* Chetham Society OS. Vol.XXIII, (1857). p.40.

15 R. K. Field, 'Worcestershire Peasant Buildings, Household Goods (etc.)', in *Medieval Archaeology.* Vol.9. (1965). pp.105–145.

16 Similar fireplaces are in the Cross Keys near Saddleworth Church (1745) and 23a King Street, Delph (1764).

17 Raines Mss Vol.2 fol.58. For a study of George Shaw see G. B. Howcroft, *George Shaw of St. Chad's, Saddleworth.* 1972.

18 J. Bradbury. *Saddleworth Sketches.* (Oldham). 1871. p.208.

19 Raines Mss Vol.1 fol.214.

20 B. Barnes, et al. (1983).

21 Foundation stones have been revealed at Woolleys, Greenfield.

22 A Wrigley. (1912). 'The Homestead' p.94. Wrigley's comments on Saddleworth houses show a sympathetic appreciation of their essential qualities.

23 Ibid.

24 The quarries on High Moor supplied flagstone.

25 *Saddleworth Historical Society Bulletin.* Vol.15. (1985). p.47. (Hereafter S.H.S. Bull.)

26 S.H.S. Bull. Vol.6 pp.53–55. List of Datestones.

27 Lancashire Record Office, (hereafter L.R.O.) Glebe Terrier.

28 Raines Mss Vol.2 fol.146.

29 C. Giles (1986). S. Pearson (1985). passim.

30 The three-light window on the north side dates from 1972.

31 L.R.O. WCW. Will of Thomas Shaw of Lane. 1774.

32 S.H.S. Bull. Vol.15 p.16.

33 W. J. Smith. 'A Place in History'. *Pennine Magazine* Vol.6 No.3 (1985).

34 Notably at number 8 Oldham Road, Uppermill.

35 Photograph by courtesy of Peter Fox of Uppermill.

36 John Woolley held a lease on the property from 1720–1740. S.H.S. Bull. Vol.10 p.32–33.

37 I am grateful to Michael Buckley for copies of the Hearth Tax Returns from the original lists in the Public Record Office.

38 J. Thirsk, (ed). (1985). Vol.I. p.4.

39 J. Radcliffe. (1887). pp.483–485.

40 There is another 'wool wall' at Field Top, Holly Grove.

41 L.R.O. WCW. Will of Edmund Buckley, 1718. Further extracts are given below.

42 *Halifax Antiquarian Society.* (1950). pp.52 and 53.

43 'Philander' (S. Andrew), (1984).

44 C. Giles. (1986). passim.

45 L.R.O. WCW. Will of Robert Mayall of Shelderslow. 1721. There is a possibility that this room was a dairy.

46 On the rear extension of the hall at Townley Hall, Burnley, built circa 1725, water-shot coursing was used.

47 W. B. McKay. (1938). pp.44–45.

48 *Pennine Magazine,* op.cit.

49 West Yorkshire Archive Service, Wakefield. Registry of Deeds. P 406 533.

50 J. Radcliffe, Mss., 'Doorheads'. Hewkin Collection, Uppermill Library.

51 Title Deeds, by courtesy of Christopher Ruddy.

52 L. Caffyn. (1986) p.11.

53 Originally known as Gravemakers, the Courts Baron were held there from 1745.

54 M. T. Wild. (1971). pp.214–232.

55 L.R.O. WCW. Will of John Buckley of Overhouse, Grasscroft, 1710.

56 Note the relationships between the windows and floor levels at the Manor House, Grasscroft, just yards away. This lack of planning between stairs and staircase windows is to be seen at Salisbury Farm, Newton by Bowland, (late seventeenth century) and Matshead, near Garstang (1703).

57 Another example is at the rear of Knott Hill, Delph. (1771).

58 See P. Smith, 'The Long-house and the Laithe-house: a Study of the House and Byre Homestead in Wales and the West Riding' in I. Foster and L. Alcock, *Culture and Environment.* (1963). pp.428–436.

59 A. Wrigley. (1912). pp.19–21.

60 Wellhead on Heights Lane is another example.

61 J. M. Hunt. *S.H.S. Local Interest Trail No.9. Dobcross.* (Saddleworth) 1987.

62 E. Crane. (1983). pp.117–185.

63 B. Barnes. et al. (1983).

64 K. G. Ponting: (1970). P. Hudson: (1986). pp.25–46. E. Kerridge (1985). pp.14–59.

65 W. B. Crump & G. Gorbal. (1935). pp.60–66. C. Aspin & S. D. Chapman. (1964).

66 A. Wrigley. (1912). 'The Homestead', p.96.

67 W. Radcliffe. (1828). p.66.

68 A. Wrigley. (1912). pp.191–203.

69 These can be seen in the Colne Valley Museum, Golcar, West Yorkshire.

70 A. Quinney. (1986). pp.66–67.

71 A. Wrigley. (1912). p.97.

72 J. Aikin. (1795). p.558.

73 F. A. Latham. *Timber Town.* (Liverpool). 1967. pp.1–7.

74 A. Wrigley. (1912). p.133. A drawing by H. Blackburn based on this photograph appears in P. Bentley. (1947). p.37.

75 Evidence from the Township Map, 1822. This is fully reproduced in B. Barnes et.al. (1983). Other references to '1822' mean the building in question does or does not appear on the Township Map.

76 This was later increased to forty-four cottages by the addition of four back-to-back cottages to the east end of the row. From the tusking on the gable end of the row there was provision to extend the number of cottages if necessary.

77 A. Clifton-Taylor & A. S. Iveson. (1983). pp.108–110.

78 S.H.S. Bull. Vol.7. p.56.

79 D. Cruikshank & P. Wyld. (1975). passim.

80 D. Gurr & J. M. Hunt. *The Cotton Mills of Oldham.* (Oldham). 1985.

81 S.H.S. Bull. Vol.9. p.81.

82 A. Wrigley. (1937). p.165.

83 S.H.S. Bull. Vol.9. p.77.

84 L.R.O. WCW. Wills of the Buckley family.

85 For an evaluation of James Gibbs and his influence see T. Friedman. *James Gibbs.* (1984).

86 S.H.S. Bull. Vol.15. p.55.

87 B. Barnes. (1981). p.49.

88 Examples can be seen in the following works:
    A. Adburgham. *Shopping in Style.* (1979).
    H. Hobhouse. *A History of Regent Street.* (1975).
    J. Summerson. *Georgian London.* (1945).

89 Illustrated in T. Farmer *Bygone Saddleworth.* (Saddleworth). 1971.

90 Pigot & Co's *Directory of Yorkshire*, 1828.

91 S.H.S. *Local Interest Trail No.9. Dobcross.* 1987.

92 G. B. Howcroft. (1972). passim.

93 For correct pointing of stone buildings see, *The Care and Conservation of Georgian Houses.* 1978. pp.82 and 83, and also Gilbert William, 'Pointing Stone and Brick Walling'. *S.P.A.B. Technical Pamphlet No.5* 1979.

Bibliography

Saddleworth Historical Society Bulletin. Vol.1 (1971) – Vol.16 (1986).

SADDLEWORTH HISTORICAL SOCIETY. *Local Interest Trails.* No's 1–9.

C. ASPIN & S. P. CHAPMAN. *James Hargreaves and the Spinning Jenny.* Helinshore. 1964.

(S. ANDREW) PHILANDER. *A Manufacturer's Business a Hundred Years Ago.* 1984. Reprinted for Oldham Chronicle 1879.

J. AIKIN. *A Description of the Country from Thirty to Forty Miles around Manchester.* (1795)

O. ASHMORE. *The Industrial Archaeology of North-West England.* 1982.

A. N. ALCOCK. *Cruck construction. An introduction and catalogue.* 1981. (CBA Research Report No.42.)

E. BAINES (ed. K. Pontria) *Baines' Account of the Woollen Manufacturers of England.* 1970.

M. BERG. *The Age of Manufacturers 1700–1820.* 1985.

B. BARNES. *Saddleworth Heritage.* Saddleworth. 1974.

B. BARNES. *Passage through time.* Saddleworth. 1981.

B. BARNES, P. M. BUCKLEY, J. M. HUNT & A. J. PETFORD. *Saddleworth Surveyed.* Saddleworth. 1983.

P. BENTLEY. *Colne Valley Cloth.* Huddersfield. 1947.

J. BOTTOMLEY. *Greenfield: A Poem.* Manchester. 1816.

R. W. BURNSKILL. *Illustrated Handbook of Vernacular Architecture.* 1972.

R. W. BURNSKILL. *Houses.* 1982.

R. W. BURNSKILL. *Timber building in Britain.* 1985.

J. BUTTERWORTH. *History of Saddleworth.* Oldham. 1828.

L. CAFFYN. *Worker's Housing in West Yorkshire 1750–1920.* 1986.

E. CRANE. *The Archaeology of Beekeeping.* 1983.

D. CRUIKSHANK & P. WYLD. *London: The Art of Georgian Building.* 1975.

A. CLIFTON-TAYLOR & A. S. IVESON. *English Stone Building.* 1983.

W. B. CRUMP & G. GHORBAL. *History of the Huddersfield Woollen Industry.* Huddersfield. 1935.

D. G. EDWARDS (ed.). "Derbyshire Hearth Tax Assessments, 1662–70." *Derbyshire Record Society Vol.VII.* 1982.

GEOLOGICAL SURVEY OF GREAT BRITAIN. *The Country around Holmfirth and Glossop.* 1933.

C. GILES. *Rural Houses of West Yorkshire, 1400–1830.* 1986.

H. HEATON. *The Yorkshire Woollen and Worsted Industries.* 1920.

D. HEY. *Yorkshire from AD 1000.* 1986.

A. J. HOWCROFT. *Tales of a Pennine People.* Oldham. 1923.

P. HUDSON. *The Genesis of Industrial Capital. A Study of the West Riding wool textile industry c.1750–1850.* 1986.

E. KERRIDGE. *Textile Manufacturers in Early Modern England.* Manchester. 1985.

E. MERIER. *English Vernacular Houses.* 1975.

R. MUIR. *The Stories of Britain.* 1986.

D. NEWTON. "Aspects of Historical Geography in the Saddleworth Area of South-West Yorkshire." BA Dissertation. Durham. 1971.

W. B. McKAY. *Building Construction, Vol.I.* 1938.

S. PEARSON. *Rural Houses of the Lancashire Pennines, 1560–1760.* 1985.

A. GUINNEY. *House and Home.* 1986.

J. RADCLIFFE (ed.). *Saddleworth Parish Registers.* Vol.I 1887, Vol.II Uppermill, 1891.

W. RADCLIFFE. *Origins of the New System of Manufacturers commonly called Powerloom Weaving.* (Stockport) 1828.

A. B. REACH (ed. J. Ginswick). *Labour and the Poor in England and Wales, 1849–1851.* Vol.1. 1983.

W. J. SMITH. "The Architecture of the Domestic System in South-East Lancashire and the Adjoining Pennines" in S. D. Chapman (ed.) *The History of Working-Class Housing.* 1971.

J. T. SWAIN. *Industry before the Industrial Revolution: North-East Lancashire c.1540–1640.* 1986.

J. THIRSK (ed.). *The Agrarian History of England and Wales, 1640–1750.* Vol.5 1985.

R. C. N. THORNES. *West Yorkshire. 'A Noble Scene of Industry'.* 1981.

J. B. WHITTOW. *Landscapes of Stones.* 1986.

M. T. WILD. *'The Saddleworth Parish Registers'.* Textile History. Vol.I. 1971.

A. WRIGLEY. *Songs of a Moorland Parish.* Stalybridge. 1912.

A. WRIGLEY. *The Wind Among the Heather.* Stalybridge. 1916.

A. WRIGLEY. *Saddleworth Chronological Notes.* 2nd Edn. 1941.

A. WRIGLEY. *Over the Hills and Far Away.* Stalybridge. 1931.

Index

Note: Figures in bold refer to illustrations in the text.